Embroidering Animals
with Color and Texture

Dedication

For my bunnies. I truly am blessed beyond measure. Thank you, reader, for picking up this book and supporting my work. I welcome your questions and feedback.

Embroidering Animals with Color and Texture

Landauer Publishing, www.landauerpub.com, is an imprint of Fox Chapel Publishing Company, Inc.

Project Team
Managing Editor: Gretchen Bacon
Acquisitions Editor: Amelia Johanson
Editor: Christa Oestreich
Designer: Leslie Hall
Step-by-Step Photographer: Jessica Long
Project Photographer: Mike Mihalo
Proofreader & Indexer: Jean Bissell
Shutterstock used: MRizly (11 middle), Paleka (30–44 border)

ISBN 978-1-63981-116-8

Library of Congress Control Number: 2024950861

To learn more about the other great books from Fox Chapel Publishing, or to find a retailer near you, call toll-free 800-457-9112, send mail to
903 Square Street,
Mount Joy, PA 17552,
or visit us at www.FoxChapelPublishing.com.

We are always looking for talented authors. To submit an idea, please send a brief inquiry to acquisitions@foxchapelpublishing.com.

Printed in China
First printing

Embroidering Animals with Color and Texture

25 Cute Critters with Pop-Up Details and Stumpwork

JESSICA LONG

Landauer Publishing

Contents

INTRODUCTION, 6

Part 1: Starting Your Menagerie, 8

1 MATERIALS AND SUPPLIES, 10

2 GETTING STARTED, 17

3 STUMPWORK TECHNIQUES, 24

4 STITCH GUIDE, 30

5 FINISHING YOUR WORK, 47

Part 2: Critter Projects, 50

HOW TO READ THE PATTERNS, 52

6 EASY BEGINNER ANIMALS, 55

Bluebird Sampler, 56
Seahorse Sampler, 62
Dolphin Waves, 66
Peaceful Doves, 70
Fish Mosaic, 73
Beetle Collection, 78

7 CONFIDENT BEGINNER CREATURES, 83

Striped Gecko, 84
Rainbow Snake, 90
Wild Fern Deer, 94
Bumblebee Bouquet, 98
Forest Elk, 103
Mountain Bear, 107
Ringtail, 110

8 BEGINNER THREAD PAINTING CRITTERS, 116

Penguin Family, 117
Festive Feathers, 124
Monarchs in Love, 130
Desert Coyote, 134
Magic Snail, 137
Crowned Meerkat, 142

9 THREAD PAINTING A MENAGERIE, 148

Axolotl Aquarium, 149
Blue Dragonfly, 156
Raccoon and Wild Roses, 160
Berry Patch Bunny, 165
Tufted Titmouse Wreath, 170
Posing Piglet, 176

PATTERNS, 182

INDEX, 206

ABOUT THE AUTHOR, 208

Introduction

I'm so excited to share another book of animal embroidery designs with you! Since the release of *Animal Embroidery Workbook* in 2020, I've continued to explore hand embroidery techniques to capture the beauty of the natural world using fiber art. I've pushed beyond my regular stitch repertoire for the projects in this book, incorporating more dimensional embroidery stitches and stumpwork techniques. I think you will really enjoy these fun 3D designs!

The first part of the book includes information about tools and supplies along with a stitch guide. You will find step-by-step direction for techniques that will be used throughout the projects, such as pattern transfer, stumpwork, working with beads, felt and wool padding, and wire slips. The remainder of the book is packed with 25 animal embroidery projects. They are generally organized by level of difficulty but do not need to be worked in order.

Stumpwork: Embroidery techniques that create a 3D element, such as raised stitches, felt bases, and wire slips.

If you are a beginner to hand embroidery, I suggest you begin with a smaller project from the first section of designs (such as the Bluebird Sampler) to build up confidence and familiarize yourself with basic hand embroidery techniques and stitches. If you are new to thread painting, try out some of the animals in Chapter 8 before diving into the critters in the final chapter.

I hope that you find the following projects fun and relaxing. Please feel free to change the suggested stitches and colors to create something you love. You can even combine and resize elements that you like from multiple projects into a unique fiber art project. Using simple supplies, we can create lovely art through this relaxing craft. Don't take any of it too seriously—it's just hand embroidery!

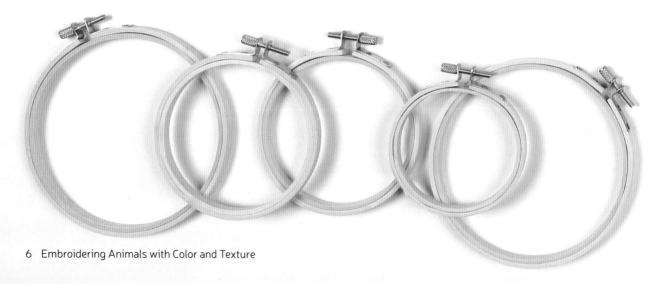

Part 1

Starting Your Menagerie

Before diving into the animal projects, please take some time to review these initial pages. Starting out with the right tools, materials, and techniques will give you the necessary information to create beautiful animal embroidery art. This is also a great section to refer to as you work through the projects.

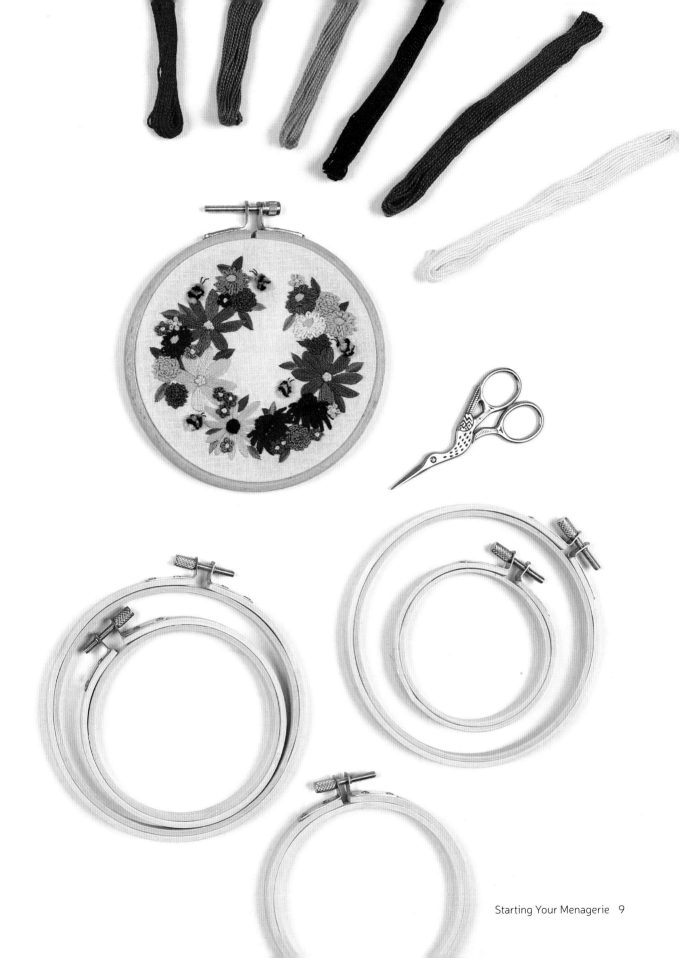

Chapter 1

Materials and Supplies

Embroidery Fabric

A wide variety of fabrics can be used for hand embroidery. Explore a local fabric store and experiment with different weaves, blends, and colors to see what fabrics you enjoy working with. Quilting cotton, linen, linen blends, silk, felt, and organza are all popular embroidery fabrics. I enjoy stitching on a simple quilting cotton, such as Kona® Cotton from Kaufman Fabrics. When I want a heavier fabric with a little more texture, I use a linen blend, such as Kaufman's Essex line of fabrics.

Double up thin or light-colored fabrics if you prefer a thicker feel and want to avoid seeing the back of the stitches through the front of your work. Doubling up also provides more stability to support wire slips. Pair stretchy fabrics with a fabric stabilizer to avoid pattern warping and wrinkles.

I frame most of my finished embroidery work in a hoop, so I do not prewash the fabric and I only need a piece of fabric 2"–3" (5.1–7.6cm) larger than my hoop size. If your finished embroidery work will get washed regularly (as part of a quilt or on clothing), prewash your fabric to avoid shrinkage and color bleeding. If you plan to frame your finished embroidery work on a canvas or if you will be using it in another project (like a pillow, book cover, or quilt), be sure to stitch on a large enough cut of fabric.

We will get an opportunity to work with sheer fabric for stumpwork in Chapter 9. You can find organza and tulle in different weights and colors at your local fabric store. It can help to see these fabrics in person to decide which cut is best for your project. I looked for a very sheer fabric with some shine to replicate insect wings. I also made sure that the weave would be both tight and strong enough to support my stitches. It can be worth trying a sample of sheer fabric types to see which works best for you. Because this fabric is transparent, it is important to hide thread anchors and the back side of your stitches, so they are not seen from the front.

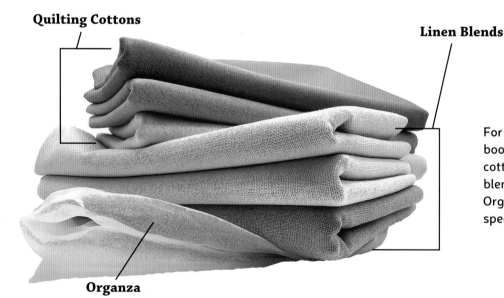

Quilting Cottons

Linen Blends

Organza

For the projects in this book, I used quilting cottons and linen blends for the base. Organza is used for specific stumpwork.

Hoops and Stands

Using a quality embroidery hoop with good tension will prevent any puckering or creasing of your fabric and give you a more stable surface to stitch through. Hoops come in many different sizes and are often made of wood or plastic. It is important to use a nice embroidery hoop for stitching, but cheaper hoops can be great for framing your finished work. I use beechwood embroidery hoops with brass fittings. They have a notch in the screw that allows for extra tightening using a screwdriver.

Beechwood embroidery hoops with brass fittings are my go-to.

An embroidery design may specify what size of hoop to work in, but sometimes it can be worthwhile to use a different size. Smaller hoops may be more comfortable to hold, and they can also provide better tension, but they will need to be moved around the fabric to reach all corners of the design. A larger hoop can be useful when a design extends beyond the edge of the designated hoop size. Those far edges can be more easily stitched before transferring the fabric back to a smaller hoop for framing.

Some stitchers prefer to use a hoop stand or clamp to secure their work, so they can stitch using two hands. Many varieties are available, including floor and table models. I use a simple 360 table vise as a hoop clamp to hold my work steady when I'm creating video tutorials, but I prefer to stitch without it.

Embroidery stands can save your hands from gripping the hoop.

Embroidery Floss

To stitch the animal designs in this book, we are using six-stranded cotton embroidery floss, which is a thread made of six divisible strands of cotton. These strands can be used individually, kept together as a whole six strands, or grouped for any number in between. Using more strands of thread will result in greater dimension and texture, while working with fewer strands will allow for greater detail and precision.

Six-stranded embroidery floss is available in hundreds of colors, including some variegated varieties that we will use in a handful of patterns in this book. For most of the projects in the book, I used DMC floss. The DMC color numbers are included in the instructions for each pattern. Use these numbers to recreate my color choices exactly, or substitute with other colors or thread brands and types. There are lots of other floss brands (such as Lecien COSMO and Anchor) and other fun floss materials (silk, wool, linen) to experiment with. Conversion charts for major thread brands can be found online.

Six-stranded embroidery floss comes in a rainbow of colors.

Find an organizational method that works for you, helping to keep your thread labeled and free of tangles. Some threads are extremely close in color, so it is important to accurately identify them before you begin stitching. Many stitchers like to wind their floss on bobbins, but there are many different ways to store and organize your thread collection.

Be familiar with the colorfastness of your thread to avoid any bleeding of colors if you plan to get your work wet. Red colors and overdyed threads are especially notorious. Wash these fibers before working with them, or plan to keep your work dry.

Variegated and metallic six-strand embroidery floss add extra color and sparkle to embroidery work.

Specialty Floss

I used variegated threads from both DMC and COSMO (labeled Color Variations and Seasons respectively) for the projects in this book. Variegated colors are usually unique, with no perfect substitutions or conversions between brands. The good news is that hand embroidery does not need to be perfect, so substitute any colors that you love if you cannot find the exact hues referenced in the patterns. Many variegated threads have a repeating pattern of colors. You can choose to match up this pattern between lengths of thread as you stitch or choose to not worry about it, letting fate decide the flow of colors.

We will get an opportunity to use metallic floss in Blue Dragonfly (page 156). Metallic threads are usually made from polyester or a polyester blend, so it can feel stiffer and be a little more challenging to work with. Use short stitch lengths and be patient. The results will be worth it.

Embroidery Needles

Hand embroidery needles, sometimes called crewel needles, have a sharp tip and a streamlined eye. They are usually available in sizes 1 through 10, with 1 having the largest eye (to be used with thick threads or many strands of floss) and 10 having the smallest eye (to be used with a single strand of floss). Grab a couple of variety packs of hand embroidery needles to have a good assortment of sizes to handle one through six strands of thread. Note that there can be differences in needle size between brands.

Your needle size will depend on your design, what stitches you are using, how thick your threads are, and your own personal preference. Play and see what feels good in your hands. A large needle makes a bigger hole in your fabric and reduces accuracy, but it is easier to thread. Smaller needles help with precision and detailed thread painting, but they can be challenging to thread. I generally use the smallest needle I can comfortably thread, and I readily bump up a size if I am experiencing any frustration.

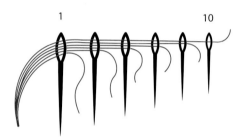

Keep assorted needle packs on hand, since different sizes work better with different strand counts.

I organize my needles by size on a labeled pincushion.

Other Needles and Notions

- **Beading needles** are great for attaching beads to your work, but small embroidery needles can be used instead.

- **Milliner's needles** are useful for knotted stitches (like French knots and bullion knots) and beading. Their eyes and shafts are the same width, so they won't get stuck when pulled through a tight wrap or bead.

- **Chenille needles** have much larger eyes, so they can be easier to use with thicker threads. Some stitchers prefer using chenille needles instead of embroidery needles.

- A **large darning needle** is a great tool for sinking the tails of wire slips into your project fabric. Any needle with a large enough eye for the wire tails to slip through can be substituted.

- A **long straight pin** is useful for the open-based picot stitch. Any long needle can be substituted.

- **Pincushions** and **magnetic needle minders** can help keep your needles organized and safely stored.

- **Needle threaders** are a useful tool to help you squeeze floss through miniscule needle eyes.

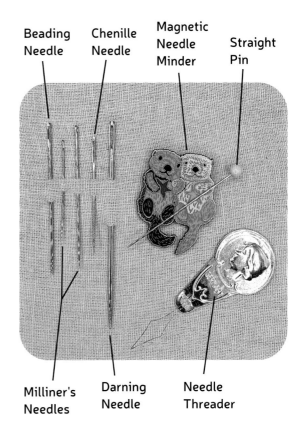

Beading Needle · Chenille Needle · Magnetic Needle Minder · Straight Pin · Milliner's Needles · Darning Needle · Needle Threader

Not every needle or notion is required, but I suggest testing these options to see what styles and accessories you prefer.

> ## TIP
>
> If you can't find a large enough eye when working with all six strands, try this trick. Cut a double length of floss and pull out three strands. Thread these strands through your needle's eye, and stitch with the doubled-over length—now six strands thick!

Stumpwork Supplies and Tools

Stumpwork requires additional materials that aren't typically used in surface embroidery. Here are some of the supplies you may use, whether for beadwork, raised embroidery stitches, or wire slips, which allow you to create detached elements.

Wire

Cotton-covered wire, commonly used for flower arranging and cake decorating, works well for creating detached embroidery elements. Thinner wire, such as 34 gauge, is a great choice for more delicate or smaller pieces like insect wings. Thicker wire, such as 32 or 30 gauge, will give more stability to flower petals, leaves, and bird wings.

When choosing a wire gauge, find a balance between strength and visibility. Thicker wires will be better at holding a shape but will be easier to spot, creating a thick border around your detached element. Thinner wires will be less noticeable along the edges of the slip, but they may be too weak to maintain their shape without drooping from the weight of the fabric and stitching. Green cotton-covered wire works well for leaves. White cotton-covered wire can be colored with an archival ink pen to match the color of your thread.

Padding

Felt and loose wool are both great options for padding. Felt is a thick fabric created from pressed synthetic or natural (wool) fibers, or a mix of the two. It can be easily cut, attached, and layered onto your project fabric. Using a pattern, felt fabric can be cut into very specific shapes to be covered with hand embroidery stitches.

Loose, or roving, wool is not pressed or woven. Rather, it is lightly processed, loose clumps of fiber sheared from an animal, such as a sheep. It can be formed by hand and attached to fabric to create more dramatic volume than felt, but its lack of weave or structure requires extra anchoring stitches. Loose wool is more moldable than felt fabric, but the loose fibers can be more challenging to contain under embroidery stitches.

Wire Tools

- **Needle-nose pliers** are useful for shaping wire. While wire is easily shaped by hand, pliers are especially handy for creating shapes with sharp points.

- **Heavy scissors** or **wire cutters** are important for trimming the wire.

- **Small, sharp scissors** should be used to accurately cut the wire slips from the fabric.

- **Fabric glue**, carefully applied with a paintbrush or cotton swab, is useful for securing frayed fabric along the wire slip edges.

- **Large-eyed needles**, such as darning needles or chenille needles, can be helpful for inserting wire slips into the main project fabric.

Beads

Stitch beads with your hand embroidery work for some extra color, sparkle, and variety. I used size 11 round seed beads for some of the projects in this book. Beads come in many other different sizes, shapes, colors, materials, and finishes. Pretty much any bead can be incorporated into your work, though some may require more care than others.

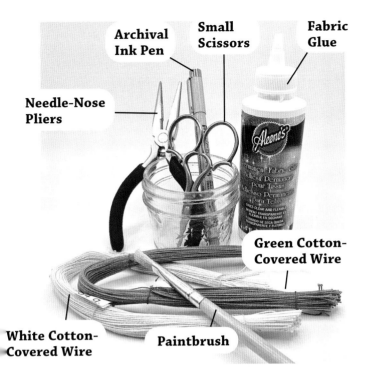

Needle-Nose Pliers

Archival Ink Pen

Small Scissors

Fabric Glue

Green Cotton-Covered Wire

White Cotton-Covered Wire

Paintbrush

Wire maintains the shape and structure of detached details.

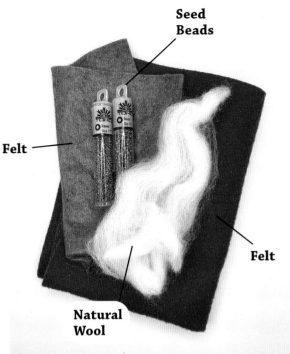

Seed Beads

Felt

Felt

Natural Wool

Spice up any embroidery project by adding padding and beads.

Transfer Tools

To create the projects in this book, you need to transfer the designs to your fabric. Here are the tools I use most often for the light tracing method, which will be discussed more on page 21. Fabric and sewing shops are full of the helpful tools and products mentioned here, but using a pen from your junk drawer and a bright window to trace your design can work just as well.

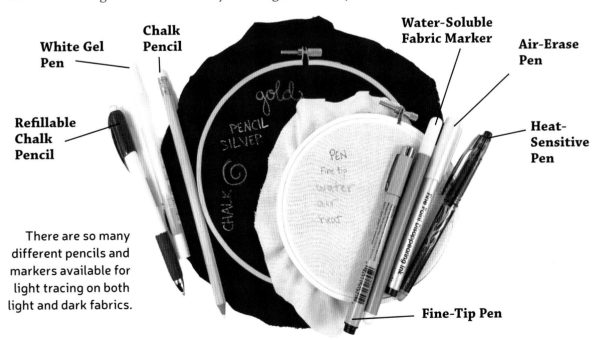

White Gel Pen

Chalk Pencil

Water-Soluble Fabric Marker

Air-Erase Pen

Refillable Chalk Pencil

Heat-Sensitive Pen

There are so many different pencils and markers available for light tracing on both light and dark fabrics.

Fine-Tip Pen

- **Water-soluble fabric markers** are great for this tracing method, but remember that your embroidery will need to be rinsed upon completion to remove the guidelines.

- Any **permanent marker** or **pencil** can be used to trace if your guidelines will be completely covered by stitches. Archival, acid-free inks are the best option when considering the long-term effects of the pens on your embroidery work.

- A **heat-sensitive pen** (such as FriXion® pens from Pilot) can create guidelines that can be erased with a blow dryer or iron. They are not specifically designed for fabric use, though, so do use with caution.

- A **chalk pencil** or **white gel pen** (such as Sakura Gelly Roll®) is best when working on dark fabrics. Lines made by chalk pencils can either be washed or rubbed away, but they might also be accidentally rubbed away during your work. Gel pens leave permanent marks that will need to be concealed with your stitches.

- A **light board** is a great tool for transferring patterns to fabric. Most boards have a clear plastic surface with a bright light underneath. An embroidery pattern is secured to the board and the project fabric is placed on top. The board creates a sturdy, flat surface for tracing, and the bright light helps illuminate the pattern guidelines through the fabric. When shopping for a light board, look for one with bright lights and a large enough board size to fit your projects. You can use a bright window instead, but some people prefer the horizontal tracing surface of a light board.

Other Supplies

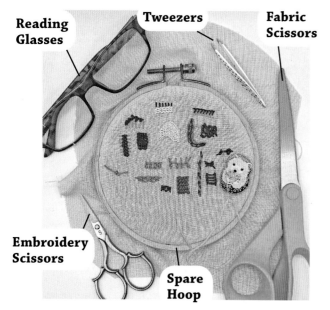

Reading Glasses

Tweezers

Fabric Scissors

Embroidery Scissors

Spare Hoop

Keep these specific tools on hand for when you need them, which is often more than you think!

- **Tiny embroidery scissors** with small, sharp blades are important for cutting lengths of floss and for trimming threads from your work.

- **Larger fabric scissors** are great to have for prepping your fabric and cutting felt for padding.

- **Tweezers** are useful for removing stitches.

- **Lint rollers** are perfect for cleaning up thread bits and for dusting finished embroidery art.

- A **spare hoop** fitted with scrap fabric can be kept nearby to practice stitches. This hoop is like a scratch pad or sketch book. It's a place to work through ideas and techniques before trying them on a project hoop.

- Use **reading glasses** or other magnification if needed.

Chapter 2

Getting Started

Take Care

Care for your eyes and body. Stitch with plenty of light, appropriate glasses or other magnification, and a comfortable seat. Take regular breaks during marathon stitching sessions.

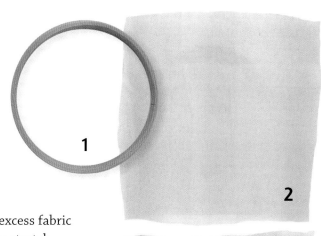

Hoop Up

If you plan to use your hoop as a frame for the finished piece, leave 1"–2" (2.5–5.1cm) of excess fabric to cinch back upon completion. If you plan to stretch your embroidery on a wooden frame or canvas, make sure you leave yourself enough excess fabric for that purpose. If you will not be framing your work in a hoop, be sure to remove your work from the hoop after each stitching session to avoid permanent creases in the fabric.

1. Sandwich your fabric between the inner and outer embroidery hoops. Start by placing the inner (smaller) hoop flat on the table. The inner hoop is the bottom bread of our sandwich.

2. Center the fabric over the inner hoop. This is our fabric filling.

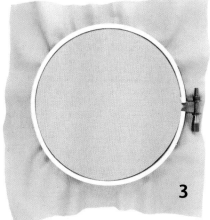

3. Place the outer hoop (the top bread) on top. Tighten the screw and pull the edges of the fabric out evenly from the center, moving clockwise around the hoop.

4. Repeat until you reach your desired tension. Notice how the hoop looks now after multiple rounds of tightening the screw and pulling the fabric edges out. There should be no wrinkles in your fabric. You want your fabric to be drum tight—that is, as taut as the surface of a drum—to avoid puckering and warping of the design.

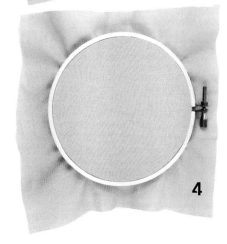

Thread the Needle

Pull floss from your skein from the end marked with the color number. Cut a piece of floss no more than 24" (61cm) long to avoid tangles. Your pattern will let you know how many strands to use, one to six, depending on the design and style. If needed, separate the individual strands of floss by pulling them out individually from the cut length. Use one hand to pull out a single ply (strand) and gently hold the remainder of the strands in your other hand.

"Sharpen" the end of your floss with a lick and a snip of your embroidery scissors for easier threading. Be sure to use a needle with a large enough eye. If you are struggling with threading, try jumping up a needle size or using a needle threader.

Note the individual strands that make up a full six-stranded cotton floss. Refer to the pattern to determine how many strands to use. Cut a working length from the skein before separating the strands.

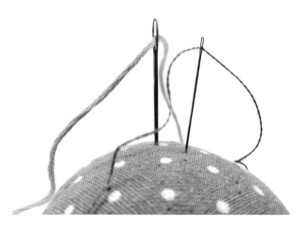

You will thread a larger needle for a full six strands of floss.

MAKE MISTAKES

Make mistakes. Don't be afraid to start over or to remove your needle and pull up some stitches. You can use the tip of your needle to pull up stitches, but a pair of tweezers and embroidery scissors can be handy when things really go wrong. It's okay—embroidery is about the process. Just keep practicing and give yourself a break.

Oops! I had to perform "surgery" on this loose French knot. I used my embroidery scissors to cut the knot and my tweezers to help pull out the trimmed threads.

How to Bind a Hoop

I bind my embroidery hoops to ensure that my fabric is pulled tight as I stitch. Just a strip of fabric can increase a hoop's effectiveness. Binding with wider strips will be faster and require a shorter strip length, but they may be too bulky and bunch up when wrapped around the tighter curves of smaller hoops.

1. Cut scrap fabric into 2"–3" (5.1–7.6cm) **wide strips.** The required strip length will depend on the size of the hoop you wish to bind and how thick you want your binding to be. A 6" (15.2cm) hoop may need 36"–72" (91.4–182.9cm) fabric length, depending on the strip width and desired binding thickness. Strips longer than 24" (61cm) can be cumbersome to wind. Work with multiple strips if needed.

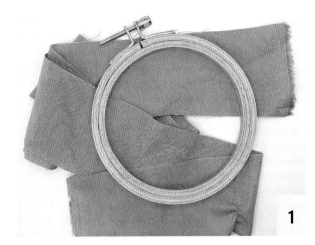

2. Begin winding the fabric around the inner embroidery hoop. Each wind of the fabric will overlap and secure the bound section before it. Keep the fabric as smooth as possible as it overlaps itself. Increase the amount of overlap to build up a thicker bind.

3. Continue winding the fabric around the hoop. Stop when you return to where you began binding. Overlap the start by a couple of winds, and cut away any excess length of the fabric strip.

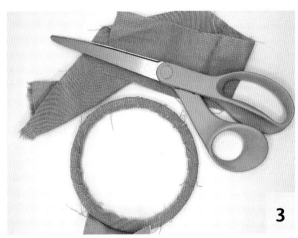

4. Secure the tail of the binding to the beginning of the binding. Use the full thickness (six strands) of embroidery floss and a few running stitches.

5. Tie the two ends of the thread to secure. Trim the thread tails and any extra fabric to tidy up the binding. I usually just bind the inner hoop, but for extra grip, both the inner and outer hoops can be bound.

4

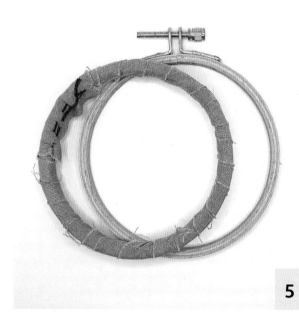

5

PRINTED DESIGNS

To purchase fabric printed with the designs from this book, please visit www.JessicaLongEmbroidery.com.

Light Tracing Transfer

The key to a successful project is a neatly transferred embroidery design. It can be tempting to rush this somewhat boring step, but I encourage you to take the time to do it right before picking up your needle and thread. Before using a specialty fabric pen or pencil, be sure to read the instructions thoroughly and test on scrap fabric first.

I utilized this transfer method for every design you see in this book. Simply use the light from a bright window, lamp, or light board to trace your design to the fabric. This method works best for lighter fabrics where light can easily shine through. If using thinner dark fabrics, use a chalk pencil or white gel pen. See more transfer methods on page 22.

1. Copy the appropriately sized design. Trim so it fits on the back side of the embroidery hoop.

2. Hoop up the fabric. Tape the design to the back of the fabric, within the inner embroidery hoop. The fabric needs to be drum tight.

3. Hold up your hoop to a bright light and trace the design. Trace slowly and take breaks when transferring large designs. I used a water-soluble marker here.

4. Confirm every part of the design has been traced. Remove the printed pattern from the back of the fabric.

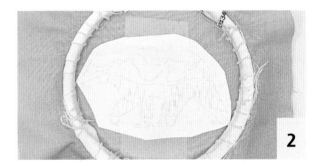

- -

TIP

Alternatively, tape the design and unhooped fabric directly to a window or light board for tracing. The traced design can warp slightly after hooping up the fabric, so I prefer hooping up first.

- -

OTHER PATTERN TRANSFER TECHNIQUES

The best technique for you is going to depend on a number of factors, all of which are touched upon in the following chart. Ultimately, there may be multiple solutions to your pattern transfer "problem," and it will be up to you to decide which method works best for you. Just remember to test your transfer method and its permanence before you begin.

Heat and Carbon Methods

Iron-on and carbon transfer methods are great for darker and thicker fabrics when light will not shine through. You'll need to purchase specialty papers and pencils, so be sure to follow the instructions that come with your products. These methods are often permanent, so you'll need to cover the guidelines completely with your stitches.

Stabilizers

Printable stabilizers are another great option for thicker fabrics and garments. Simply print your design from your computer onto this paper and stick it on your fabric. This method saves time and sanity when transferring large, complicated patterns and is perfect for people who hate to do any tracing. Always test your fabric first, as this method can leave behind a halo or adhesive that is difficult to remove.

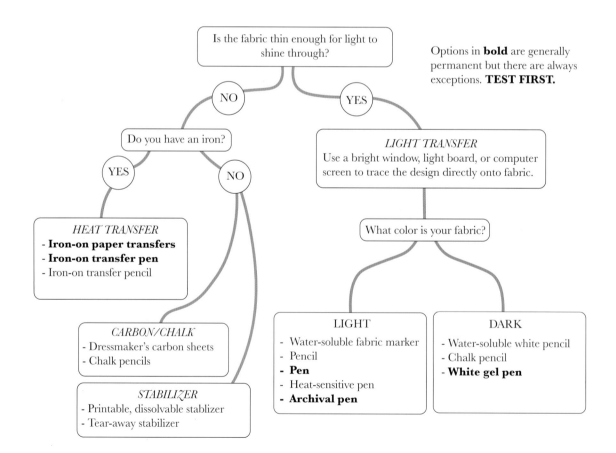

Anchor Your Floss

Preventing your embroidery from unraveling is super important, especially if your final piece is something that will get a lot of wear and tear, like clothing. However, if your embroidery is just going to be sitting pretty on wall, then anchoring may not be as important.

The basic anchoring method can be done with the following easy steps. Other popular anchoring options include the anchor knot and away waste knot. You could also keep it simple with a basic overhand knot tied at the end of your thread before you get started.

1. Start your first stitch. Hold a tail (1"–2" [2.5–5.1cm]) of floss under the embroidery with a finger while making the first stitch. Do not pull it up through the front. (This and all shots show the back side of the hoop/fabric.)

2. Anchor down the tail. Maneuver the tail so that it is tacked down by the underside of the next few stitches as you proceed with your work.

3. Secure your floss. This is done before you run out of threaded floss (when only a couple of inches [5.1cm] of floss remain on your needle). Weave it into the underside of your stitches to secure it. Keep the back side of your work as neat as possible and trim any excess tails.

4. Continue from the previous anchor. Subsequent lengths of thread are easier to anchor by weaving into the back of your previous stitches.

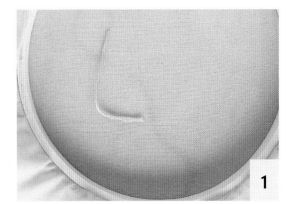

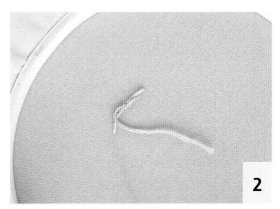

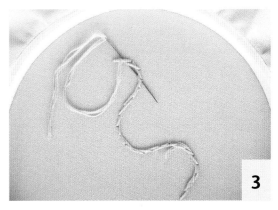

Chapter 3

Stumpwork Techniques

To add extra dimension to the embroidery projects in this book, we will be using a variety of stumpwork techniques. General techniques are described below, but additional details and variations are included throughout the projects in the book. Find traditional stumpwork stitches (such as Turkey work, trailing, and other raised stitches) as well as other embroidery stitches in the next chapter.

Beads

Beads add fun dimension, color, and texture to hand embroidery projects. Use a small embroidery needle or a beading needle threaded with a single strand of thread to attach beads to your work. Match the thread to the bead color or use a contrasting color of thread if you want the stitches to be more noticeable. Beads can be secured face up, with their hole visible, or can be stitched down on their sides.

To attach a bead face up, use two small stitches. Come up through the center of the bead with your needle and go back down through the fabric on the right side. Steady the bead face up and repeat, bringing the needle back down on the left side.

To attach a bead on its side, simply add it to a small straight stitch. Come up through the fabric and through the bead with your needle; go back down through the fabric a bead-length away. When attaching a line of beads on their sides, you can use multiple beads per straight stitch. If too many beads are attached by a single stitch, the line may get droopy, so use a series of shorter lengths instead.

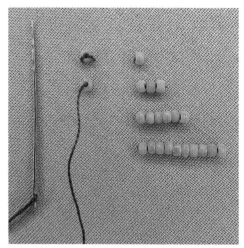

Beads can be attached face up (left) or they can be secured on their sides (right). Add them to any project for some extra dimension or sparkle.

Padding

Felt and wool can be attached to the project fabric to create extra dimension. Felt can be layered to build up extra volume, and wool can be stuffed under those layers for even more dramatic results. Wool can be manipulated and shaped into forms that may be too complicated to cut from felt. Use your best judgment when deciding the best padding material for your project.

Layering Felt Padding

1. Cut out the paper template to use as a stencil. Trace as many shapes as needed onto the felt and cut them out.

2. Secure using small straight stitches. Use a single strand of thread to attach the felt where desired on the main project fabric. If layering multiple pieces of felt, attach the small piece first.

3. Attach any larger felt pieces in a similar manner. This layering creates a smooth and consistent effect for the padding. Surface embroidery work can be stitched directly on top of these felt layers.

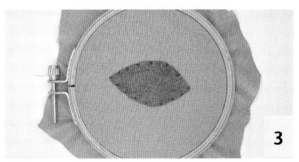

4. Keep the straight stitches small and very close to the felt edges. Make as many of these stitches as needed along the perimeter of the felt to secure it to the project fabric.

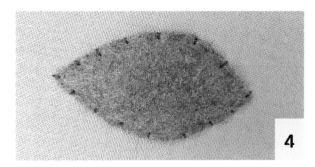

Attaching Wool Padding

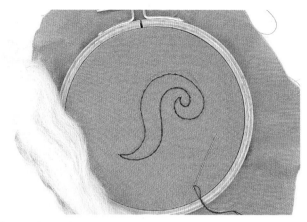

1. Outline the edge of the padded shape. Use a split stitch and a single strand of thread.

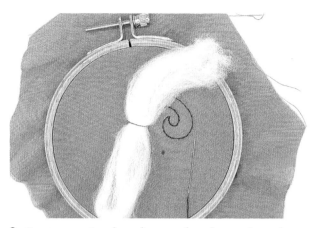

2. Center a strip of wool over the shape. Loosely secure it to the main project fabric with a straight stitch.

3. Add more straight stitches over the wool. Work toward one edge of the shape. Use various angles, and keep a steady tension to avoid creating creases in the padding form.

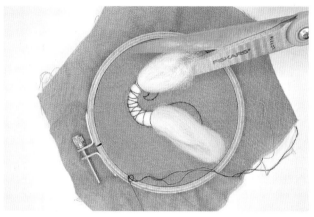

4. Cut away any excess padding. This is anything that extends beyond the outline stitched in step 1.

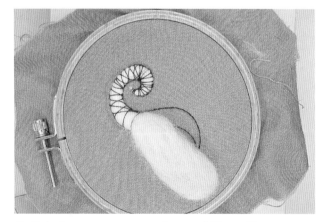

5. Continue to secure the padding. Use straight stitches and fit within the shape outline.

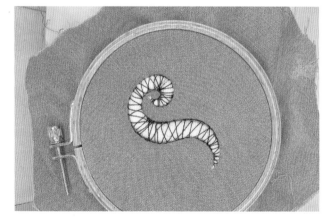

6. Review the final profile of the shape. Add additional stitches to secure and sculpt the form as needed

Wire Slips

Wire slips are detached elements that add dramatic dimension to embroidery projects. They are created on a second cut of fabric that is secured in an additional hoop, separate from the main embroidery project. Once stitched and cut out from this second hoop, they are inserted into the fabric of the main project. Projects with wire slips will have a pattern for the main project fabric and a pattern for the detached element fabric. Usually, the stitching on the main project fabric should be completed first before attaching the wire slips.

Creating Wire Slips

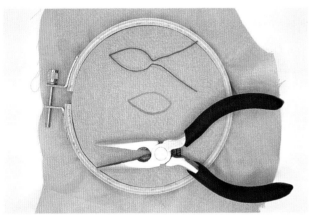

1. Cut a length of wire longer than needed.
Roughly mold it to match the shape of the detached element pattern. You may find it helpful to use needle-nose pliers for sharp corners. Trim the tails of the wire so they are 1" (2.5cm) long, and direct them to edge of hoop, away from other wire slips.

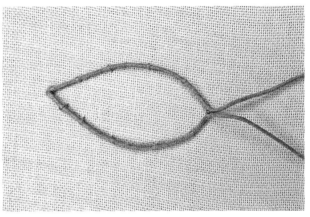

2. Couch (page 34) the wire to the fabric.
Use a single strand of thread. This step secures the shaped wire in place for the next step.

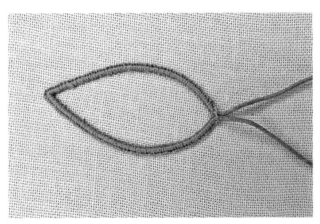

3. Completely cover the wire. Use a single strand of thread and a buttonhole stitch.

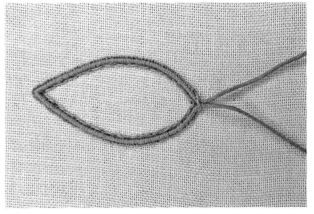

4. Tightly outline the buttonhole stitch.
Use a split stitch and a single strand of thread.

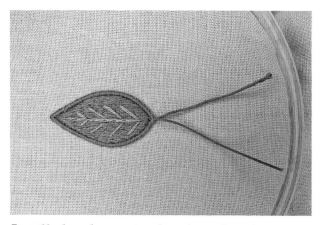

5. Fill the shape. Stitch as desired or fill as indicated in the pattern instructions.

6. Remove the detached element fabric from the hoop. Carefully cut the wire slip from fabric. Use your fingers to rub the edges of the slip to fray any remaining fabric fibers. Trim these fibers.

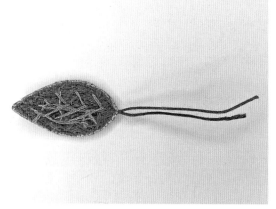

7. Trim any thread tails on the back of the work. If desired, apply fabric glue using a paintbrush to any wild tails on the back and edges of the wire slip.

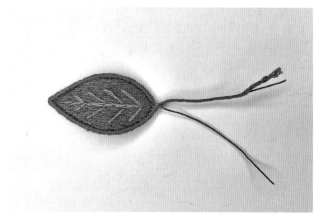

8. If using cotton-covered wire, remove the covering from the wire tails. This makes them easier to insert into the main fabric. Use caution, as this wire can now potentially rust and stain your work. You can choose to keep the cotton on the wire.

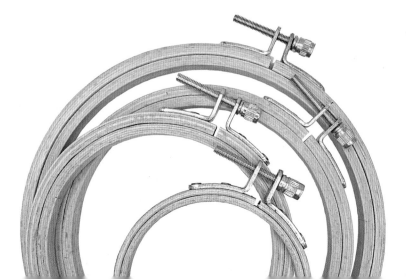

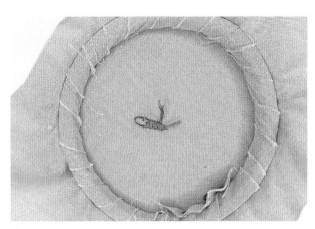

9. Insert a large needle (such as a darner) into the main fabric. Place so that the eye is at the surface of the fabric. Thread the wire tails of the stumpwork piece through the eye of the needle. Pull the needle through to sink the wires.

10. Bend the wire tails in half. Secure them to the back side of the main fabric using straight stitches and any thread. Hide these stitches under the wire slip, or secure to the back of other stitches rather than stitching through the main fabric.

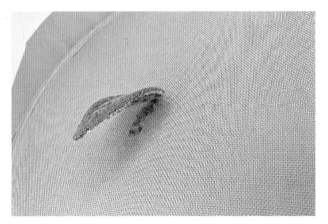

11. Check the stitches from the front. They should be hidden behind the wire slip.

12. Gently shape the slip on the front side of the main project fabric.

Chapter 4

Stitch Guide

It's important to learn and practice individual stitches before beginning an embroidery design. Included in this section are all the stitches you will need to know to create any of the designs in this book, as well as a discussion of thread painting. This guide is intended as a quick reference. You can also go to my website for video tutorials of these stitches.

TIP

Looking for a fun way to learn hand embroidery stitches and explore the relationships between them? I've also created Hand Embroidery Companion Cards, which include 30 unique stitches and a set of embroidery stitch samplers. A diagram, written instruction, tips and tricks, a photo, and a QR code linking to an online video tutorial are included on each. The cards are also marked with symbols indicating their relative difficulty, their stitch family, and their stitch use. Learn more here:

Hand Embroidery Stitches

Stitches are listed alphabetically. Sometimes, a more complicated stitch is listed before the basic version. For example, attached fly stitch is listed before the fly stitch. When other stitch names are referenced within a description, they are shown in **bold** to indicate that you can look for them within this stitch guide.

Attached Fly Stitch

Begin with a **fly stitch** on a long anchor stitch. Come up through the fabric at A, and back down a horizontal stitch length away at B, leaving a loop. Come up at C, and tack the loop down at D to create a fly stitch. Continue from A on a new fly stitch, creating a chain of touching stitches to create a vine.

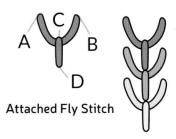

Attached Fly Stitch

Back Stitch

Back stitch is a simple stitch for creating lines and vines. Start a stitch length away from the beginning of the line. Come up at A, then down at B, which is the start of the line. Come up a stitch length away at C, and back down at A. Up again at D, then down at C. Continue in a line, being sure to go up and down through the same holes so there is no gap between the back stitches.

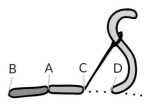

Back Stitch

Back Stitch Fill

There are many ways that can be used to fill a shape with **back stitch.** If using rows (left diagram), begin with a center line to establish a consistent stitch direction. To create a shape with a crisp edge, outline with back stitch first before spiraling in to fill towards the center.

Back Stitch Fill

Back-Stitched Chain Stitch

Begin with a row of chain stitches from A to B. Add a row of **back stitches** on top, from A to B, ending and beginning a new stitch within each chain.

Back-Stitched Chain Stitch

Blanket Stitch

Blanket stitch is a traditional edging stitch that creates a line with regular vertical stitches. Come up at A. Go back down at B one stitch length above the guideline and one stitch length away, leaving slack. Come up at C, a stitch length away from A, and catch the loop from the first stitch. Continue in the same manner: go down at D, leaving slack to catch when coming up at E. End with a small **straight stitch** anchor.

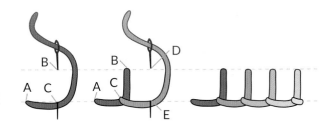

Blanket Stitch

Buttonhole Stitch

Fill a shape using closely worked **blanket stitches** (left diagram). Alternatively, begin the row of blanket stitches with a loop as if starting a **chain stitch** (right diagram), which avoids the small bump created by the first blanket stitch. Working the stitches on a diagonal can be helpful for filling shapes with pointed ends, such as leaves. Choose to keep the blanket stitches parallel with each other or vary the angle while filling the shape.

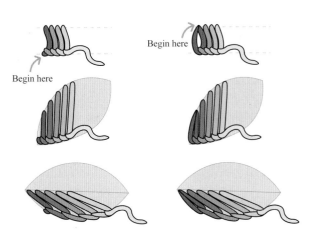

Buttonhole Stitch

TIP

I use buttonhole stitch to secure wire when making wire slips. I like to begin on the inside of the shape with the chain stitch start.

Chain Stitch

Come up and down with the needle at A, which is the start of the line, leaving a loop. Come back up within the loop at B, a stitch length away. Pull to tighten the loop to desired tautness. Continue, ending the chain with a small **straight stitch** to tack down the final loop at C.

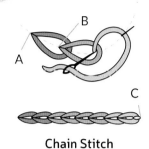

Chain Stitch

Chain Stitch Fill

There are many ways to fill a shape with chain stitch. One option is to fill a shape with **chain stitches** using straight, parallel rows (left diagram). Another is to fill with rows that follow the contour of the shape (right diagram). When using straight rows, begin with a center line to help establish a consistent stitch direction. When following the contour, begin with the outlines to create a crisp edge, and then work toward the center.

Chain Stitch Fill

Chain Stitch Rose

Begin with a center stitch, such as a **French knot**, to establish a point to spiral out from. Use the **chain stitch** to fill the space, beginning at the center and moving out, eventually filling the shape. Keep the stitches small, especially during the tighter parts of the spiral near the center. Play with tension to change the texture of the rose.

Chain Stitch Rose

Checkered Chain Stitch

Checkered chain stitch creates a fun chain of alternating colors. Begin with two colors of floss threaded through the eye of the needle and come up at A. Insert the needle through the fabric from A to B, keeping one color below and one color above the needle tip. Pull the needle through (making a **chain stitch**) and repeat, inserting from B to C and keeping the other color below the needle tip. Pull through and continue to create a chain. Finish at D with a small **straight stitch** using both colors, anchoring the final chain.

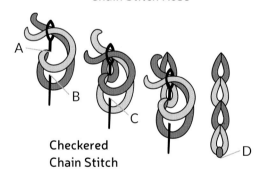

Checkered
Chain Stitch

TIP

If you struggle with the alternating method described in Checkered Chain Stitch, you may find it easier to recreate this stitch using two threaded needles instead.

Colonial Knot

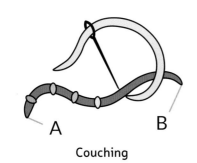

Couching

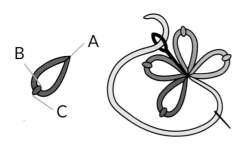

Detached Chain Stitch

Colonial Knot

Come up from the fabric, letting the thread lie loosely to the right, creating an arch. Bring the needle tip under the arch so that the thread rests over the needle from left to right. Use a free hand to pull the working thread to the left and back over the tip of the needle, creating a figure eight with the thread. Start bringing the needle back down through the fabric near the original hole, and pull the wrapped figure eight to the fabric surface. Push the needle through the wrap and the fabric to complete the knot.

Couching

The couched thread is pulled up at the start of the line at A and goes down at the end of the line at B, leaving slack. The couching thread is then used to tack down the couched thread along the curves of the line. Both threads are anchored once the desired line is created. This stitch uses two working threads, which can vary in thickness, type, and color. Couching is a great linear stitch for lettering and for creating stems or vines.

Detached Chain Stitch

Come up with the needle at A and go back down the same hole, leaving a loop. Catch that loop at B, a stitch length away, and tack down the loop at C. Play with stitch length and experiment with tension, creating a thinner or more rounded shape. Combine multiple detached chain stitches that share a center point to create a lazy daisy (right diagram).

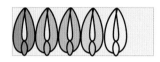

Detached Chain Stitch Fill

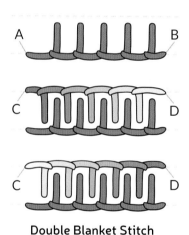

Double Blanket Stitch

Detached Chain Stitch Fill

Fill a shape with rows of **detached chain stitches**. Line the stitches up parallel to each other (top diagram) or create them at variable angles to better fit the shape (bottom diagram).

Double Blanket Stitch

Create a line of **blanket stitches** from A to B. Make a second line of blanket stitches from C to D or from D to C. Turn the fabric upside down to create this second line of blanket stitches to avoid having to work the stitch backward or upside down. Space the stitches so that the vertical sections of each line of blanket stitches are staggered.

Feather Stitch

Feather stitch creates an interesting vine that can be modified by altering tension and stitch length. Come up through the fabric at A, and down a horizontal stitch length away to the right at B, leaving a loop. Come up at C, catching the loop, and go back down to the left at D, leaving a loop. Continue, swinging from right to left while creating connected U shapes. End with a small **straight stitch** to anchor.

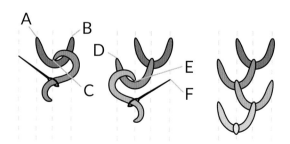

Feather Stitch

Fern Stitch

Begin with a **straight stitch** from A to B. Come up at C a half-stitch away from B, and come down at A. Complete the trio with a stitch from D to A. Repeat this triplet of straight stitches in a line to create a vine. Alternatively, create a **back stitch** "stem" first, then return down the line, adding the two straight stitches at every back stitch intersection (right diagram).

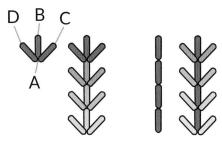

Fern Stitch

Fishbone Stitch

Begin with a **straight stitch** down the center of the leaf, reaching about one-third of the way down the shape. Use diagonal straight stitches to fill the shape. Come up on the right at A, down at B, then switch to the other side by coming up on the left at C and down at D. Continue to alternate sides, with the straight stitches crossing each other at the center line of the shape. Change the look by exaggerating the angles and modifying the distance between the straight stitches.

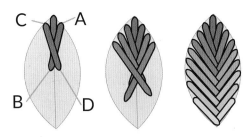

Fishbone Stitch

Fly Stitch

Fly stitch can be used for U- or V-shaped decorative accents, such as petals and leaves. Come up through the fabric at A, and back down a horizontal stitch length away at B, leaving a loop. Come up at C, and tack the loop down at D to create a fly stitch.

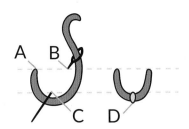

Fly Stitch

Fly Stitch Fill

Begin with a center **straight stitch** from A to B. Begin filling the shape with **fly stitches**, starting at the top and working toward the base of the shape. Filling a leaf with fly stitch creates a unique center vein made of anchor stitches. The fly stitch angle and distance between stitches can be modified to create different leaf looks.

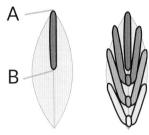

Fly Stitch Fill

French Knot

Wrap thread around the needle, then place the tip of the needle back down to the surface of the fabric, near the exit point. Pull the excess thread away and the wrapped thread down to drive it to the tip of the needle, so the wrapped thread rests on the fabric surface. Push the needle through to complete the knot. Practice by wrapping around the needle once, as this will be the easiest knot to pull through. To change the size of the knot, wrap the thread around the needle one to three times or use a different thread thickness.

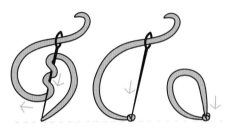

French Knot

Long and Short Stitch

Begin by creating a row of **straight stitches**, alternating between long and short lengths (A). Because this original row is staggered, all remaining rows will echo this uneven edge. Fill the second row with stitches that pierce the stitches in the original row (B). Continue filling the shape with rows of split stitch (C), modifying the length of the stitches in the final row to fit within the shape guidelines (D).

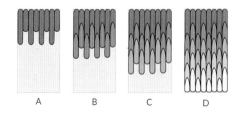

Long and Short Stitch

Long and short stitch is the most common stitch used when thread painting. Learn more on page 45.

TIP

Outline the shape before filling with the long and short stitch to get a cleaner edge and to create the illusion of overlap between objects.

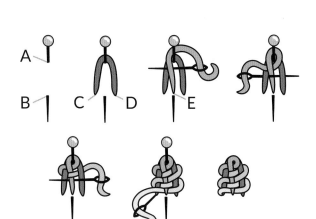

Open Base Picot Stitch

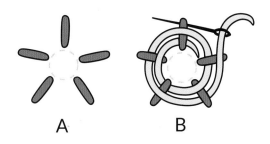

A   B

Open Woven Wheel Rose

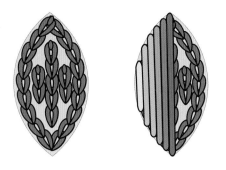

Padded Satin Stitch

Open Base Picot Stitch

Insert a pin in the fabric from A to B, the length of the finished picot stitch. Come up through the fabric at C, and loop the thread behind the pin head before going back down at D. Come up at E, loop behind the head of the pin, and slip under the same thread from right to left.

Begin to weave back and forth, using these three strands as a foundation. First weave from left to right, weaving under, then over, and under again. Returning to the left, weave over, then under, and over again. Continue to weave while maintaining sufficient tension to pack the woven thread and tightly fill the shape. Finish by coming down at C or D, depending on which side the weaving is completed, and remove the pin.

Open Woven Wheel Rose

Start with a frame of five **straight stitches**, radiating from a circular group of stitches, such as a cluster of **French knots** (A). Come up with the needle near the center stitches, and weave under and over the straight stitch spokes (B). Once the spokes are covered, bring the needle back down through the fabric.

Padded Satin Stitch

Outline the shape with a linear stitch, such as a **back stitch** or **chain stitch**. Add additional stitches inside the shape to creating padding. Cover this initial layer with the **satin stitch**, beginning with a **straight stitch** down the center line to establish a direction guideline.

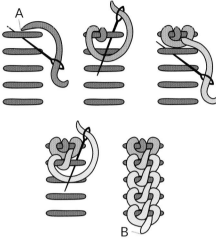

Raised Chain Stitch

Raised Chain Stitch

Begin with a column of evenly spaced, horizontal **straight stitches**. Come up at A and weave the needle under the first straight stitch from below, pulling it through to the left of A. Loop the thread toward the right, leaving slack. Weave the needle under the first straight stitch from above, on the right side of A, catching the loop and pulling through. Repeat, weaving under the second straight stitch from below and pulling through toward the left. Finish at B to secure the final loop.

Raised Stem Stitch

Begin with a column of evenly spaced, vertical **straight stitches**. Come up at A at the lower-left corner of the shape. Weave under the first vertical straight stitch from right to left, and gently pull the slack, allowing the wrap to rest along the bottom of the shape. Next, weave under the second vertical stitch from right to left. Continue weaving under every straight stitch, bringing the needle down at B once reaching the bottom-right corner of the shape. Come back up at C and repeat, creating another row before coming back down at D. Add as many rows as needed to fill the shape.

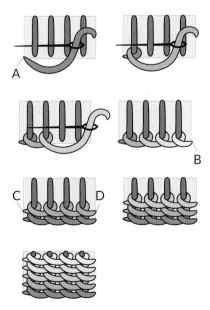

Raised Stem Stitch

Reverse Chain Stitch

Start at the "end" of the chain with a small **straight stitch** from A to B. Come up through the fabric a stitch length away at C. Slip the needle under the anchor stitch (do not pierce the fabric) before coming back down through the same hole (C). Continue in a chain. Some people prefer reverse chain stitch over **chain stitch**. The resulting embroidery work is the same but may vary slightly in in tension due to how the stitches are performed.

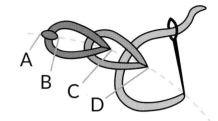

Reverse Chain Stitch

Running Stitch

Come up at A and down a stitch length away at B. Continue, coming back up at C and down at D, creating a dotted line. This is a quick linear stitch traditionally made with evenly spaced, even-length stitches.

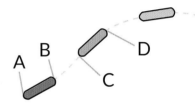

Running Stitch

Satin Stitch

Fill the shape with **straight stitches**, starting with a center stitch from A to B. Continue to fill the shape with parallel straight stitches, maintaining a consistent stitch direction. Go slow and experiment with tension to keep the stitches smooth and evenly spaced with no gaps. Using fewer strands of floss will result in smoother texture.

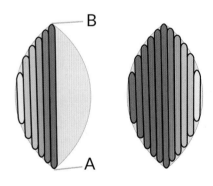

Satin Stitch

Sorbello Stitch

Begin with a **straight stitch** from A to B. Come up at C, directly below A, and weave under the original stitch from above. Pull the slack through toward the left. Weave under the original stitch from above again, this time staying to the right of the first weave. Keep the tip of the needle over the loop, and pull the slack toward the right. Bring the needle down at D to finish.

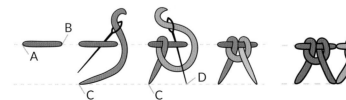

Sorbello Stitch

Split Stitch

Begin with a **straight stitch** from A to B. Pierce this stitch from below, coming up at C and going down a stitch length away at D. Continue making a line. If splitting the previous stitch from below is too challenging, try a split back stitch: come up through the fabric a stitch length away at D, and go back down through the middle of the previous stitch at C.

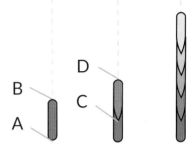

Split Stitch

Split Stitch Fill

Fill a shape using rows of **split stitches**. To fill with a consistent stitch direction (left diagram), begin with a center guideline, then continue to fill the shape in rows to either side. Alternatively, use the edge of the shape to determine the stitch direction (right diagram). Begin with an outline of half the shape, then work rows going toward the center before repeating on the other side.

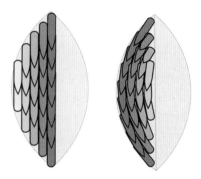

Split Stitch Fill

> ### TIP
> Begin all rows at the same side of the shape.
> Use fewer strands for a more consistent texture.

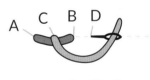

Stem Stitch

Stem Stitch

Come up at A and down at B, leaving the stitch loose below the guideline as the needle goes back up at C. Pull the slack from the first stitch, then go back down at D and up at B, keeping that stitch loose below the needle. Continue, going down at E and back up at D. Alternatively, keep the thread above the needle to create a line with a twist in the opposite direction.

Stem Stitch Fill

Use rows of **stem stitches** to fill a shape. To fill with straight rows, begin with a center line, then fill each half in rows to either side (left diagram). To match the stitch direction to the shape's contour, outline one edge to guide the remaining rows (right diagram).

Stem Stitch Fill

Straight Stitch

Also called a stab stitch. Come up at A, and go down at B. Vary length, direction, and quantity to add some spice to this basic stitch building block.

Straight Stitch

Tapered Trailing

Begin to cover the base threads as with regular **trailing**. Thread the end of one base thread on a needle. Bring it to the back of the fabric at A, the point where tapering will begin. Continue to cover the remaining base thread (or threads) with small **straight stitches**. Near the end of the guideline, thread the end of the remaining base thread on a needle, and bring it to the back of the fabric at B. In the same manner, complete the trailing toward the other end of the guideline.

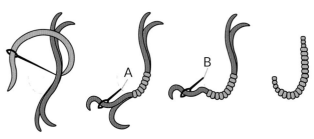

Tapered Trailing

Trailing

Select a quantity of base threads, each 6" (15.2cm) or more longer than the length of the guideline. Secure the base threads using small **straight stitches** that come up and down through the fabric tight to the guideline. Begin somewhere near the center of the line and work toward one end, keeping the small straight stitches tight together so that the base threads are completely covered.

   As you near the end of the guideline, thread the ends of base threads on a needle, and bring them to the back of the fabric at A. Depending on the thickness of these threads and the quantity, you may need to thread them one at a time. Continue to cover the base threads with small straight stitches to the end of the guideline. In the same manner, complete the trailing toward the other end of the guideline.

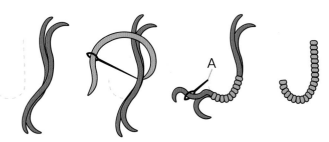

Trailing

Turkey Work

Turkey work is a fun way to add texture or fringe to designs. Start above the fabric and bring the needle down at A, leaving a tail on the top side of the work. Come up at B and down at C, covering A. Come up near A, under the **back stitch**, and back down at D, leaving a loop. Secure this loop by coming up at E and down at B, covering D. Repeat, creating loops and securing them with back stitches. Leave the loops intact or trim them.

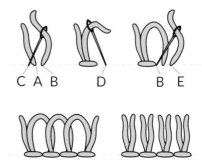

Turkey Work

TIP

Securing the loops with the back stitch makes them lie flat.
Split the stitches instead to get fringe that comes straight up from the fabric.

Wheatear Stitch

Create **straight stitches** from A to B and from C to B. Come up at D to create a **reverse detached chain stitch**, weaving under both original stitches, and go back down at D. Recreate the original two stitches, this time converging at the base of the detached chain stitch at D. The next chain stitch will weave under these straight stitches and the previous chain stitch. Continue to make a chain of stitches.

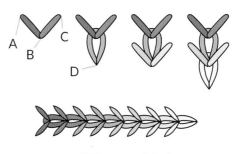

Wheatear Stitch

Wheatear Fill

Use the **wheatear stitch** to create leaves with serrated edges. Work the stitches loosely to leave delicate gaps or tightly to cover the fabric. Begin with a **straight stitch** down the center from A to B. Come up at C to create a **reverse detached chain stitch**, weaving under the original stitch. Create straight stitches from D to C and from E to C. Make another reverse chain stitch, weaving under these straight stitches and the previous chain stitch. Repeat, filling down the shape.

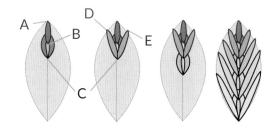

Wheatear Fill

Whipped Back Stitch

Complete working the **back stitch** line from point A to B. To whip a back stitch, come up with your needle at A, the beginning of the line. Weave under and over every stitch until reaching the end of the line. Do not pierce the fabric until bringing the needle down at B.

Whipped Back Stitch

TIP

You can also whip other linear stitches, such as the **running stitch** and **chain stitch**.

Woven Wheel Rose

Start with a frame of five **straight stitches** in the shape of a star that converge at A, the rose center. Come up near A and begin to weave under and over the straight stitch spokes. Do not pierce the fabric, just weave. Continue until the spokes of the wheel are completely covered. Bring the needle down through the fabric at the edge of the rose, and weave under the stitches on the wrong side of the fabric to secure.

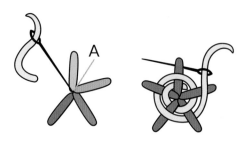

Woven Wheel Rose

Using Long and Short Stitch for Thread Painting

Long and short stitch is a method for filling a shape using rows of overlapping stitches. It is very versatile and can be used to fill a shape with a solid color or with multiple hues to create smooth color transitions and shading. Depending on the number of strands of thread and the length and direction of the stitches, this technique can result in a smooth surface or a dramatically textured look. Very realistic work can be created when using single strands of thread and many colors, so this technique is often called thread painting or needle painting.

Thread Painting Tips

Utilizing long and short stitch for thread painting is a challenging yet rewarding hand embroidery technique. Use this method to create color gradations and shading to give your subjects a three-dimensional look. The thread painting patterns in this book include suggested colors, number of strands, and stitch directions. With this knowledge in hand, you can create your own thread painting designs in the future.

The basic long and short stitch diagram shown on page 37 can be misleading when trying to fill a complicated design. For example, when stitching the penguins (page 117), I did not work from top to bottom, filling in every inch of fabric as I stitched. Sometimes I fill using one color at a time, working from the darkest color to the lightest. Other times I work by body part, starting from one end of the animal then moving to the other. The stitch order is less important than completely covering the fabric and thoroughly blending between colors. As with any other kind of painting, it is okay to add additional layers of color over previously filled sections.

When painting with thread, it is okay to return to sections to add more stitches to cover the fabric or to rework and smooth out any color transitions.

One more very important note about thread painting: Every single thread painting I have ever made always goes through an ugly phase, during which I nearly throw away my work. I promise that this is normal and that the best way to get through it is to persevere without judgment. Just keep stitching!

On page 46 are a few key tips I have discovered through many hours of long and short stitching. Use them to help you understand the design decisions that were made for the embroidery art in this book.

TIPS FOR LONG AND SHORT STITCHING

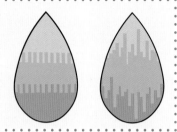

Add variety to stitch length. A blocky, perfectly measured long and short stitch is lovely, but by creating more variety in your stitch length (add extra-long and extra-short stitches), the transition between colors will look more smooth and realistic.

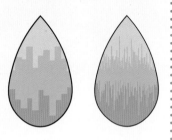

Use a single strand of floss. A thicker strand of floss will create more texture, which may be distracting or may be exactly the look you are trying to achieve. Using a single strand will be like coloring with a fine-tipped pen, a way to create controlled and delicate lines. Using a full six strands will provide faster coverage with more texture and less control, much like you would get with a thick, chunky marker.

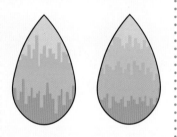

Add more shades of color. The more steps between two colors, the smoother your transition will be. Your work will be more realistic as you increase the number of colors and decrease the difference in hue between those colors. But of course, the more colors you use, the more time it will take to complete your project! Be prepared to spend hours stitching a thread painting project. Unfortunately, there are no shortcuts here.

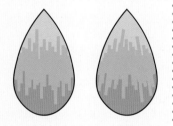

Play with stitch direction. Sometimes keeping your stitches neat and parallel with your shape is appropriate, but it can be interesting to see the variation created when you change the angles. Stitch direction can help add dimension to shapes and direct focus.

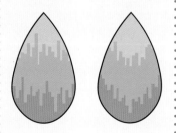

Curve color transitions. Another way to play is by making slight changes to where you transition from one color to another. Curve your shading for more realism, giving your objects a more three-dimensional look. If you are using a model, be sure to pay attention to the actual shadows. It's likely that they do something more interesting than follow along a straight line.

Chapter 5

Finishing Your Work

Finishing in a Hoop

The simplest way to finish your work is by framing it in an embroidery hoop and hanging it proudly on the wall.

Wooden hoops look nice natural, but it can be fun to stain or paint them with acrylic paint and apply a varnish. A framed embroidery in a small painted hoop with a cute ribbon makes a lovely handmade tree ornament. Pull out the glitter glue and sequins to create an extra-sparkly frame.

As an alternative to the standard hoop shape, you can stretch the finished work on wood canvas bars for a more elegant look in a rectangular frame. Line the wood with framer's tape and add an additional layer of fabric to help protect your embroidery art. Use clamps to similarly center and evenly stretch the fabric across your frame. Secure with staples or use a full six strands of embroidery floss to lace the back side to secure the work.

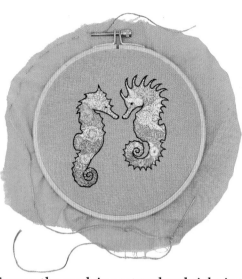

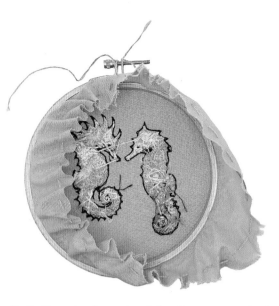

1. Ensure the work is centered and tight in the hoop. Trim any excess fabric and use a running stitch with a full six strands of floss along the entirety of the fabric edge.

2. Pull on both ends of the floss to cinch the fabric closed. Alternatively, use acid-free craft glue to secure the fabric to the inner edge of the embroidery hoop.

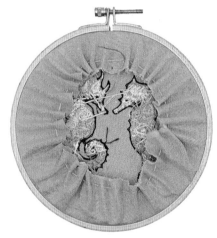

Make your own wood canvas bars or buy them precut at art supply stores.

3. Use a double knot to secure the floss and trim. The back side of the hoop can be left open, exposing the stitches, or it can be covered with fabric, felt, or cardstock for a more finished look. It's also easy to cut the running stitches out if you decide to alter your embroidery art or reframe using another method.

Staining your inexpensive wooden hoops creates a sophisticated frame for your hoop art. Use craft stain or even wood stain pens for an easy fix.

Embroidery on Clothes

Hand embroidery can be worked on your clothes, tote bags, or any other fabric you can imagine. Transfer the pattern to the material and hoop up as you would for another project. If your piece is large, you might need to move the hoop to work one area at time. However, consider the mechanics of stitching on a small or awkward part of the garment. Your embroidery hoop may not fit, and it may be challenging to reach your hand around and under some areas. It's easiest on a large, open area, such as the back of a jacket, the pocket of a shirt, or along the brim of a hat.

Hand stitching directly onto clothes can be challenging. Dark, thick fabrics can be difficult for pattern transfer, plus they may be challenging to pierce with a needle. The right tools and materials can remove some of this challenge, but it still won't be as easy as stitching on quilting cotton. Stitching on stretchy fabrics can result in warped and puckered designs if not paired with a stabilizer.

I stitched a modified version of the Bluebird Sampler (page 56) to the back of my jacket. I chose to freehand draw the design on the denim first using a thick felt pen. Another pattern transfer option is to use a dissolvable or tear-away stabilizer printed with the design.

As easy alternative to stitching directly on your garment is to make a patch. Cut out work stitched in a hoop, and make an iron-on patch (secured with extra stitches) using fusible web products found at most craft stores. This can be attached to clothes, coats, or backpacks, even in those tricker spots.

Hoops are charming, but don't feel limited in where to put your stitching.

Elevate a project framed in a hoop by installing it in a shadow box. These 3D frames are especially great for stumpwork projects, and they keep your art dust-free.

Part 2

Critter Projects

The next four chapters are filled with 25 unique animal embroidery patterns. Chapter 6 is full of easy patterns, perfect for the beginner embroiderer or for anyone looking for a quick project. Chapter 7 expands on the skills and stitches practiced in Chapter 6 with larger, more time-consuming projects and added complexity. While some stumpwork is used here, it matches the intensity of the chapter it's in, slowly introducing more complex techniques as you go.

The final two chapters explore thread painting, using long and short stitch to make your cute critters. The projects in Chapter 8 will provide a nice warm-up, with fewer colors to juggle and often using more strands of floss to help speed up filling the shapes. In Chapter 9, you will get an opportunity to use more color and to add lots of detailed thread painting with a single strand of floss, while managing more technical color placement and stitch direction. Stumpwork is used heavily in this chapter as well.

The projects in each chapter are not necessarily in order of difficulty, so tackle whichever one speaks to you!

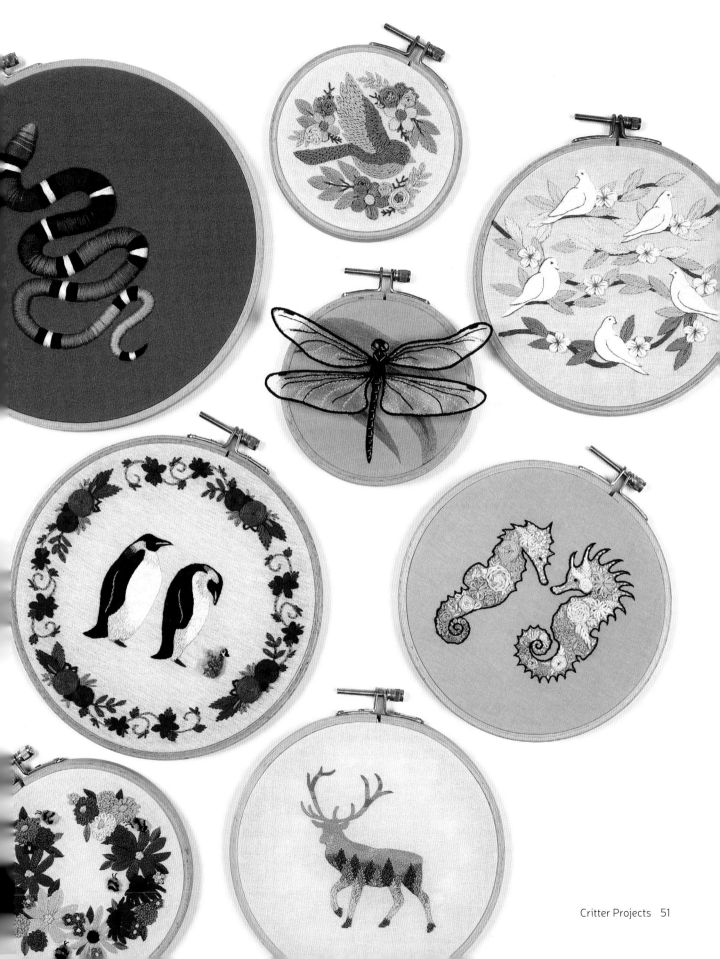

How to Read the Patterns

Each pattern includes a stitch and color key plus step-by-step instructions for stitching the design. The first project of each chapter also includes step-by-step photos to help you get comfortable with the embroidery techniques used throughout this book.

Complete color list

Step-by-step instructions   **Stitch and color diagram**

Stitch and Color Key

The stitch and color key serves as a concise reference for the pattern. The diagram includes the embroidery stitch to use for each element, plus a suggested number of thread strands and a DMC floss color. For example, the petals in the Bluebird Sampler (page 56) read "Fly stitch (6, 3778)," which means to use six strands of DMC color 3778 to create the petals with fly stitch. The given floss numbers are DMC six-stranded cotton unless otherwise stated. The included colors and strand numbers are only a suggestion and simply reflect what I used for the sample hand embroidery art.

THREAD VARIATIONS IN THE STITCH AND COLOR KEYS

Note the placement of the parenthesis in the following examples:

The center of this coneflower in Bumblebee Bouquet (page 98) is filled with French knots using six strands of thread. The French knots near the top of the flower are created with DMC color 902; the ones near the bottom are created using DMC 3371.

Coneflower
French knot center (6, 902) & (6, 3371)
Satin stitch petals (2, 304)
Straight stitch (3, 902)

The short grass in Posing Piglet (page 176) is created with straight stitches using three strands of thread. Two strands of DMC 988 and one strand of DMC 907 are combined and threaded through the eye of a needle to create a two-toned stitch. Additional short grass is created with straight stitches using three strands of DMC 987.

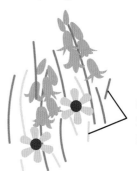

Short grass
Straight stitch
(2, 988 & 1, 907) & (3, 987)

The colors in some diagrams have been exaggerated to help avoid confusion between hues. The diagrams have also been simplified to give a general illustration of more complicated designs. Variegated thread colors are represented by a single hue.

For thread painting projects, not every little stitch or detail is captured. The placement of shade transitions acts as a guide and should not be considered hard color changes. Please see the project photos, and push stitches over the lines to create a more realistic animal.

For example, if you fill the raccoon following the diagram exactly, you will create blocky color transitions. Notice in the photo how I interpreted the diagram. There are many stitches that overlap the color transition guideline that help blend the fur to make it look more realistic. Use photos of real animals for more inspiration.

The written step-by-step instructions for the designs provide the same information as the stitch and color keys, but they also offer a suggested stitch order. I captured the order in which I tackled each project, but there are as many ways to approach a project as there are stitchers!

The diagram colors are meant as guides, not hard-and-fast rules; your colors should often have softer transitions, as you can see in the stitched raccoon.

Stitch Direction and Padding Keys

Some projects include a stitch direction key. This diagram shows you the suggested stitch direction using green lines over a simple line drawing. The pink guidelines tell you where to outline your design before filling, a technique for adding more depth to your project.

For example, let's look at the stitch direction diagram for the top axolotl from the Axolotl Aquarium (page 149). The green lines show how the long and short stitch should be placed down the body. The pink lines show where to outline the guidelines first before filling with stitches. These outlines will be covered by your fill stitches. In this example, the head and the right legs are outlined so that they appear to overlap the body. The body is also outlined where the bottom-left leg emerges to create additional depth. All these outlines are then covered by the long and short stitches used to fill the shapes.

Suggested padding placement is indicated in blue in the padding diagrams included for some projects. Use split stitch to outline the Striped Gecko (page 84), following the pink guidelines. Then apply the padding to fill the blue shape. The outline and padding are covered with stitches as described in the pattern.

When stitching your cute critters, remember that all animals in nature look different. It's okay if your designs don't look identical to mine. Biological diversity makes our planet amazing and will make your artwork amazing too.

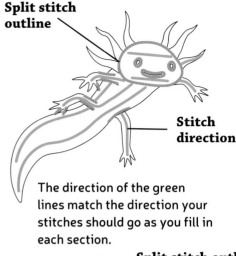

Split stitch outline

Stitch direction

The direction of the green lines match the direction your stitches should go as you fill in each section.

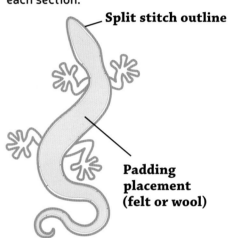

Split stitch outline

Padding placement (felt or wool)

Wool or felt padding is applied to the blue areas shown in this key.

Using and Resizing Patterns in this Book

Each project has a pattern for you to transfer to your fabric. These patterns can be found at the back of the book. Make a working copy by tracing or photocopying this pattern. Use a copy machine to resize the designs as needed.

To shrink or enlarge a design, divide the desired size by the current size of the pattern and multiply by 100%.

For example, to enlarge a 4" (10.2cm) project to fit a 6" (15.2cm) hoop: ($6/4$) × 100% = 150%

Alternatively, to shrink a 6" (15.2cm) project to fit a 4" (10.2cm) hoop: ($4/6$) × 100% = 66%

To create an easy mirror image of a design (for iron-on transfer methods), use tracing paper. Use a thick marker to trace the design and simply turn it over for the mirror image.

Chapter 6

Easy Beginner Animals

These projects are a great place to start for beginners and for stitchers looking for a relaxing project. The embroidery stitches used are beginner friendly but occasionally used in challenging ways. Look for the suggested substitutions and variations to simplify the designs.

Bluebird Sampler

This folksy bluebird pattern is a great beginner project. It's small and it features my favorite basic hand embroidery stitches. Swap in some holiday colors to turn the project into a thoughtful handmade gift or tree ornament.

Tips and ideas:
- Reuse the individual floral elements for other projects. They are cute accents that can be stitched onto clothing, backpacks, or canvas shoes.

Top of wings
Detached chain stitch fill (167)

Body
Split stitch fill (931)

Eye
French knot (167)

Wing
Chain stitch fill (927)

Beak
Satin stitch (422)

Tail
Back stitch fill (167)

Chest
Stem stitch fill (422)

Stitch Direction

	167
	422
	927
	931
	950
	3013
	3051
	3053
	3771
	3778
	3859

MATERIALS

- 4" (10.2cm) embroidery hoop

- 6" x 6" (15.2 x 15.2cm) light pink cotton fabric

- Embroidery needles, sizes 3, 6

- Cotton embroidery floss

Bluebird

Use six strands of thread for all stitches

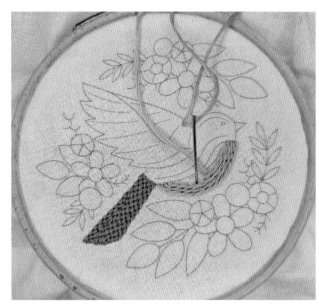

1. Fill the tail with rows of back stitch using DMC 167. Outline the bottom and top edges of the tail before filling the rows. Choose to line up your back stitches or stagger them (as pictured). Because the tail shape is flared, add extra back stitches on the wider edge of the tail to fill in the space.

2. Use DMC 422 to fill the chest with rows of stem stitch. Start near the head and outline along the belly. Continue to echo this stitch direction, starting back at the top of the shape for each row.

3. Use DMC 931 to fill the body with split stitch. Create the outline of the shape first. Continue to fill along this outline, working your way toward the center of the shape.

4. Fill the top of the wings. Use two rows of detached chain stitch with DMC 167. Begin with the top row and work from the side closest to the body out toward the wing edge. The angle of the detached chain stitches will slowly change from one side of the row to the other to fill the shape.

5. Use rows of chain stitch with DMC 927 to fill the wings. Begin at the far edge of the wing to make the first chain stitch row, starting near the top wing and stitching toward the wing tips. Continue filling with chain stitch rows using this same direction so all rows end at the wing edge. If fabric is showing through the chain stitch rows, use the split stitch to fill in any gaps.

6. Complete the bird with two finishing stitches. Create the beak with satin stitch using DMC 422. Add a French knot eye with DMC 167.

Florals

1. Fill in the daisies with satin stitch. Refer to the color key. Fill the center circle using a horizontal stitch direction and six strands. Finish by filling the petals, using six strands and a stitch direction radial from the center.

2. Fill in the roses. Refer to the color key. Choose from three stitches, using six strands of thread for each: woven wheel roses, open woven wheel roses with French knot centers, or chain stitch roses.

3. Fill the small leaves with fly stitch. Use three strands of DMC 3013. Start with a central straight stitch at the leaf tip, then fill in with fly stitches toward the leaf base. Use back stitch to make the stems.

4. Fill the larger leaves with fishbone stitch. Use three strands of DMC 3053. Use whipped back stitch for the stems, and make a small straight stitch for the leaf vein with three strands of DMC 3051.

5. Create the small vines with three strands of DMC 3051. Use fern stitch or feather stitch.

6. Fill in any gaps in the florals. Add French knots and fly stitches as desired. Use six strands of any of the flower colors. See the diagram and photo for suggested placement and colors.

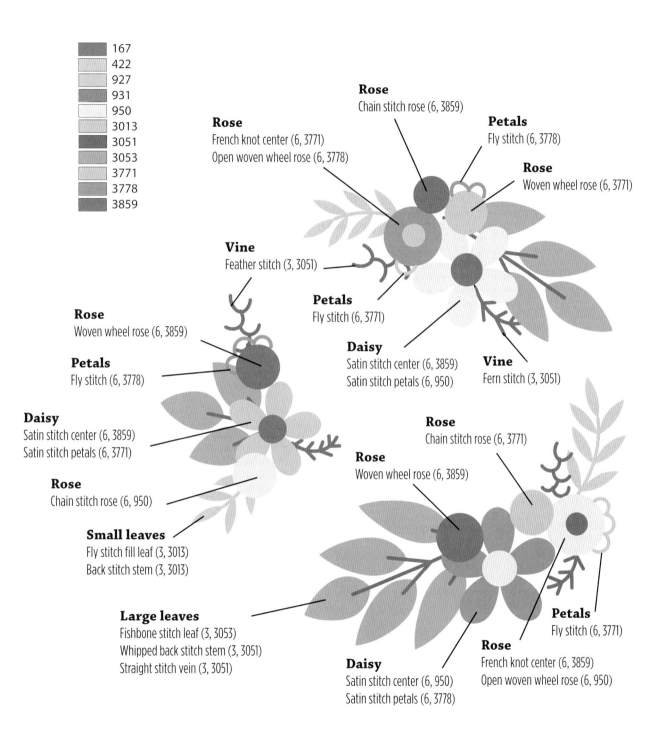

Color Key:
- 167
- 422
- 927
- 931
- 950
- 3013
- 3051
- 3053
- 3771
- 3778
- 3859

Rose
French knot center (6, 3771)
Open woven wheel rose (6, 3778)

Rose
Chain stitch rose (6, 3859)

Petals
Fly stitch (6, 3778)

Rose
Woven wheel rose (6, 3771)

Vine
Feather stitch (3, 3051)

Petals
Fly stitch (6, 3771)

Daisy
Satin stitch center (6, 3859)
Satin stitch petals (6, 950)

Vine
Fern stitch (3, 3051)

Rose
Woven wheel rose (6, 3859)

Petals
Fly stitch (6, 3778)

Daisy
Satin stitch center (6, 3859)
Satin stitch petals (6, 3771)

Rose
Chain stitch rose (6, 950)

Small leaves
Fly stitch fill leaf (3, 3013)
Back stitch stem (3, 3013)

Large leaves
Fishbone stitch leaf (3, 3053)
Whipped back stitch stem (3, 3051)
Straight stitch vein (3, 3051)

Rose
Chain stitch rose (6, 3771)

Rose
Woven wheel rose (6, 3859)

Petals
Fly stitch (6, 3771)

Daisy
Satin stitch center (6, 950)
Satin stitch petals (6, 3778)

Rose
French knot center (6, 3859)
Open woven wheel rose (6, 950)

Seahorse Sampler

This sampler offers the opportunity to practice dozens of different stitches. Fill the flowers, leaves, and vines using the suggested stitches or choose to explore completely different stitches while filling these seahorses.

I love how the eight variegated floss colors blend together and help to show off the intricate stitching within the seahorse silhouettes. These multicolored skeins can sometimes be more challenging to find than solid-colored embroidery thread. If you are unable to locate these colors, you can always use solid colors instead. Pick a rainbow of your favorite eight hues!

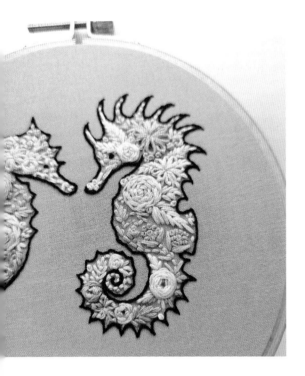

Tips and ideas:

- The project is complicated, so try to concentrate on filling the design the best you can, reducing or adding French knots and straight stitches as needed to fill the shape.

- If you are overwhelmed with indecision on what stitches to use, just pick a smaller selection of stitches to repeat throughout the project.

- Stitch the design as written or use fewer strands of thread to create a more delicate look and to allow the floral elements to decompress.

Because the colors blend well together, it is okay to diverge some from the suggested color transition points.

⬛	310
⬜	4030
⬜	4040
⬜	4050
⬜	4060
⬜	4090
⬜	4100
⬜	4215
⬜	4230

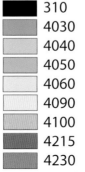

MATERIALS

- 6" (15.2cm) embroidery hoop

- 8" x 8" (20.3 x 20.3cm) aqua blue cotton fabric

- Embroidery needles, sizes 3, 9

- Cotton embroidery floss

Seahorses

Use six strands of thread unless otherwise noted

· ·

1. **Make the outline.** Use whipped back stitch with two strands of DMC 310. Fill the eyes with tiny satin stitches using the same thread.

2. **Fill in the seahorses starting at the tails.** Refer to the diagram as a guide for color placement. Work one color section at a time.

3. **Begin with the larger flowers.** For the circular flowers, use woven wheel rose stitch or fill with chain stitch roses. Use detached chain stitches to make the petals of the lazy daisies. Some of the flowers in the right seahorse are created by filling the shapes with French knots, but satin stitch can be used instead.

4. **Fill in the larger leaves.** Choose to fill each leaf with fishbone stitch, attached fly stitch, satin stitch, or wheatear stitch fill.

5. **Finish with the smaller details.** Use back stitch for vines and stems, and straight stitches for tiny leaves. Make accent petals with detached chain stitches, and create small flowers using straight stitch petals. Fill any remaining spaces with French knots and straight stitches.

Short on time? Choose to stitch a single seahorse in a smaller hoop.

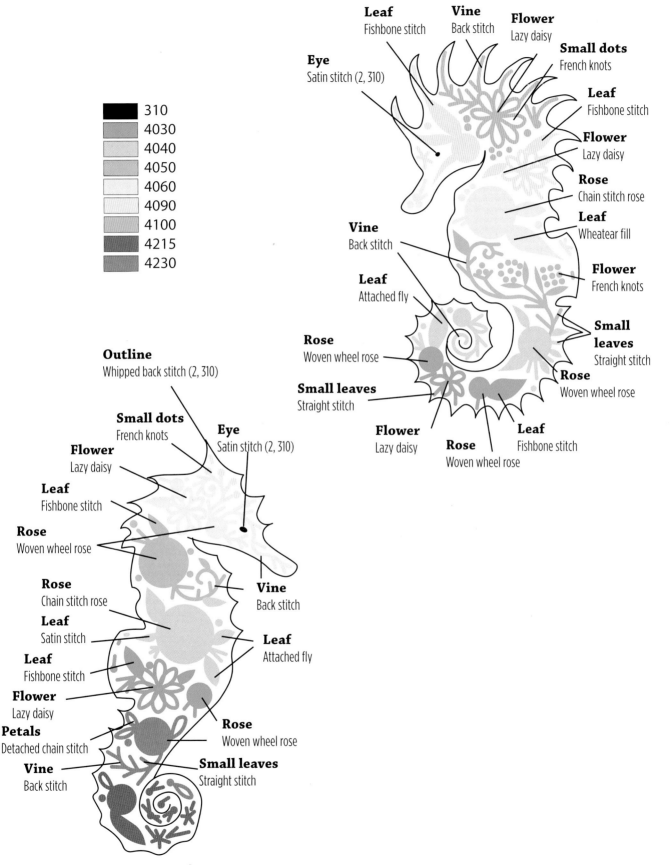

Color key:

■	310
■	4030
■	4040
■	4050
■	4060
■	4090
■	4100
■	4215
■	4230

Leaf
Fishbone stitch

Vine
Back stitch

Flower
Lazy daisy

Small dots
French knots

Eye
Satin stitch (2, 310)

Leaf
Fishbone stitch

Flower
Lazy daisy

Rose
Chain stitch rose

Leaf
Wheatear fill

Flower
French knots

Vine
Back stitch

Leaf
Attached fly

**Small
leaves**
Straight stitch

Rose
Woven wheel rose

Rose
Woven wheel rose

Small leaves
Straight stitch

Flower
Lazy daisy

Rose
Woven wheel rose

Leaf
Fishbone stitch

Outline
Whipped back stitch (2, 310)

Small dots
French knots

Eye
Satin stitch (2, 310)

Flower
Lazy daisy

Leaf
Fishbone stitch

Rose
Woven wheel rose

Vine
Back stitch

Rose
Chain stitch rose

Leaf
Satin stitch

Leaf
Attached fly

Leaf
Fishbone stitch

Flower
Lazy daisy

Petals
Detached chain stitch

Rose
Woven wheel rose

Vine
Back stitch

Small leaves
Straight stitch

Dolphin Waves

This project is inspired by the happiest, most energetic mammals in the ocean! Our dolphin is filled with a pattern of wavy rows of repeating stitches, fading from a light blue down to a dark blue. All the embroidery stitches are suitable for beginners, but this project offers an opportunity to practice them within unique, slightly challenging, guidelines.

The dolphin is filled with a repeating design of 13 rows of stitches. The color pattern also repeats, fading through five hues of blue.

MATERIALS

- 8" (20.3cm) embroidery hoop
- 10" x 10" (25.4 x 25.4cm) blue cotton fabric
- Embroidery needle, size 3
- Cotton embroidery floss

Tips and ideas:

- Use the suggested embroidery thread colors or use this pattern to work through your stash of ocean-colored thread remnants. You can organize them from light to dark or use random colors to create a unique project.

- If your stitch spacing is different than mine or if you resize the design, you may want to add or subtract rows. Some of the stitch rows are challenging to crop. I suggest substituting in rows of split stitch at the top and bottom edges of the dolphin to help fill in any odd shapes.

- Some of the stitches can be tricky to create along a wavy line. Practice them first in a straight line on scrap fabric. Substitute with other easier stitches if needed, such as back stitch, chain stitch, split stitch, or stem stitch.

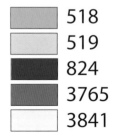

518
519
824
3765
3841

Dolphin
Use six strands of thread for all stitches

1. Organize your five thread colors from lightest to darkest. Label them Color 1 through Color 5. Begin the pattern at Row 1, the bold line on the pattern template.

2. Start with the color in the center, DMC 518 (Color 3 set). Begin with a row of chain stitch at Row 1. Follow the table, which outlines the 13 rows of stitches and colors that repeat in each set of the design. Starting in the middle of the shape establishes the wave pattern that can be then echoed above and below this guideline.

3. Move above or below and use the color set for that section. When repeating the pattern below the Color 3 set, add one to the assigned number to get the color codes for the next row. When repeating the pattern above this first set, subtract one to the assigned number to get the color codes for the previous row.

4. Continue filling the dolphin shape with rows of stitches. Crop stitches as needed to fit within the guidelines. Some waves are included on the pattern to guide you, but they do not necessarily match up with any stitch row. If needed, add more guidelines to your fabric by hand to keep your waves consistent. It is also okay if your waves shift, flatten, or change their shape as you work through the design.

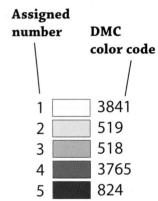

Assigned number		DMC color code
1		3841
2		519
3		518
4		3765
5		824

Colors arranged from lightest to darkest

Color 3 Set Table					
	Row		**Color**		
	Number	Stitch	Assigned #		DMC Code
One Set	1	Chain stitch	3		518
	2	Back stitch	3		518
	3	Back stitch	2		519
	4	French knots	3		518
	5	Wheatear stitch with straight stitches	2 with 3		519 with 518
	6	Back stitch	3		518
	7	Split stitch (3 rows)	2		519
	8	Back stitch	3		518
	9	Fly stitch	2		519
	10	Couching stitch	2 over 3		519 over 518
	11	Back-stitched chain stitch	3 over 4		518 over 3765
	12	Stem stitch	3		518
	13	Fishbone stitch	3		518

Cropping stitches to stay within the pattern can be challenging, especially around the irregular shape of the fins and tail. Instead of continuing with the pattern, I switched to split stitches to fill the bottom of the tail rather than trying to fit fly stitches into those small spaces.

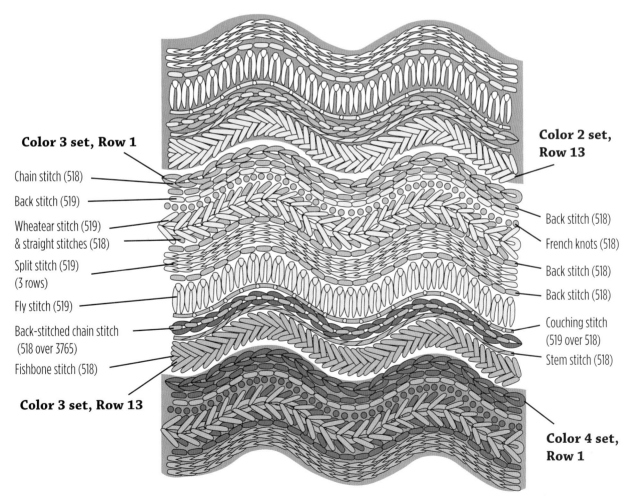

Color 3 set, Row 1

Chain stitch (518)

Back stitch (519)

Wheatear stitch (519) & straight stitches (518)

Split stitch (519) (3 rows)

Fly stitch (519)

Back-stitched chain stitch (518 over 3765)

Fishbone stitch (518)

Color 3 set, Row 13

Color 2 set, Row 13

Back stitch (518)

French knots (518)

Back stitch (518)

Back stitch (518)

Couching stitch (519 over 518)

Stem stitch (518)

Color 4 set, Row 1

Peaceful Doves

I can see our bird feeders outside of my stitching studio window. A good population of finches show up every day, but they are always outnumbered by the doves! I know they are not the most well-loved bird species, but their consistent presence and soft coos make me happy. This design features white doves and a soft, romantic color palette to match the pastel desert landscape at sunrise. Swap in some brighter hues to match your own garden or décor!

Tips and ideas:

- Many of the design's elements overlap. Sometimes it helps to stitch the element in front first, and then the element behind. You can also choose to do the opposite. Either way, there will be some back and forth between colors and elements as you work through the design.

- I created some shadow and depth to the doves by just outlining some of the birds' sides. I assigned an invisible light source to the top right of the design, so the "shadow" would not show there.

Extending the branches beyond the edge of the embroidery hoop creates an interesting detail to the project.

Stitch Direction

MATERIALS

- 6" (15.2cm) embroidery hoop

- 8" x 8" (20.3 x 20.3cm) light purple cotton fabric

- Embroidery needles, sizes 3, 9

- Cotton embroidery floss

■	317
■	581
■	644
□	739
□	819
■	3348
■	3688
■	3856
□	B5200

Doves

1. Fill the doves using two strands of B5200. Using split stitch, outline the wings first, then continue filling with split stitch while following the contour of the wing shape. Similarly, fill the body by outlining it first, then filling in.

2. Use a single strand of DMC 317 to create the eyes. Either make a single French knot or a very tiny padded satin stitch circle. If desired, continue with the single strand of 317 to outline the birds and their wing shapes with split stitch. I outlined only the bottom and left sides of each bird and wing.

3. Fill the branches with split stitch using two strands of DMC 317. Outline the branches first then fill, keeping your stitch direction parallel with the branch. If you want your branches to extend to the very edge of your embroidery hoop, stitch them while hooped up in a 7" (17.8cm) hoop. Alternatively, move the 6" (15.2cm) hoop a few times to reach these edges before rehooping with the project centered in the frame.

4. Create the flower petals. Use padded satin stitch with six strands of DMC 819. The stitch direction is radial from the center of the flower. Use a single strand of DMC 3688 to add a straight stitch stripe on top of each petal. If desired, use additional straight stitches to add more color to the petal centers.

5. Finish with the leaves. Start with a straight stitch down the center of the leaf, reaching from the tip to halfway down the length. Fill the remainder with fly stitches using two strands of thread. Follow the diagram for suggested color placement, filling roughly 10 leaves with each color. Some of the leaves are cropped by other design elements; fill these leaves with satin stitch if there is no room to use fly stitch.

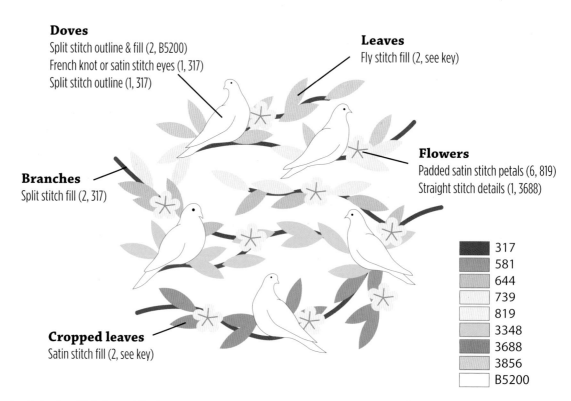

Doves
Split stitch outline & fill (2, B5200)
French knot or satin stitch eyes (1, 317)
Split stitch outline (1, 317)

Leaves
Fly stitch fill (2, see key)

Branches
Split stitch fill (2, 317)

Flowers
Padded satin stitch petals (6, 819)
Straight stitch details (1, 3688)

Cropped leaves
Satin stitch fill (2, see key)

■	317
■	581
■	644
□	739
■	819
■	3348
■	3688
■	3856
□	B5200

Fish Mosaic

I love mosaics because of their fun patterns, textures, and colors. These are the same reasons that I love hand embroidery! This project does include some beadwork. If you do not have any beads, you can use French or colonial knots instead. Substitute with some variegated and metallic threads to elevate the finished piece.

MATERIALS

- 8" (20.3cm) embroidery hoop

- 10" x 10" (25.4 x 25.4cm) blue-green cotton fabric

- Embroidery needle, size 3

- Beading needle

- Opaque-rainbow turquoise beads, round size ¹¹⁄₀

- Thread for beads in a matching color, such as DMC 993

- Cotton embroidery floss

316
334
368
437
758
3808

**Important Rows
on Pattern**

Tips and ideas:

- Raised stem stitch can be a little tricky when worked into an irregular shape. If needed, substitute with regular stem stitch to fill in those areas. Practice this stitch and any other stitches you are unfamiliar with on a scrap piece of fabric before you begin.

- Important rows are indicated on the pattern to help keep you on track. You may need to adapt the design depending on your tension, the number of threads you use, and the size of the project. Add or remove elements and rows as needed.

- If you find that the edges of your fish are uneven, you can use a back stitch outline to help to define the shape. Substitute with rows or blocks of chain stitch, satin stitch, back stitch, split stitch, or stem stitch if any of the suggested stitches are too challenging.

- I suggest using a pattern transfer method that allows you to wash the pattern from your fabric. The outlines included on the pattern are important for keeping your rows within the fish shape, but the stitches may not completely cover these guidelines, and they may be especially visible between rows of stitches.

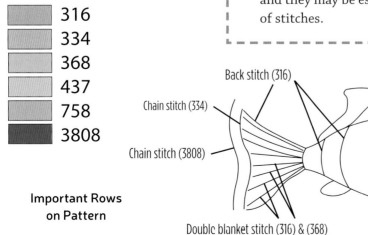

Back stitch (316)
Back stitch (316)
Chain stitch (334)
Back stitch (3808)
Chain stitch (3808)
Back stitch (368)
Back stitch (368)
Double blanket stitch (316) & (368)

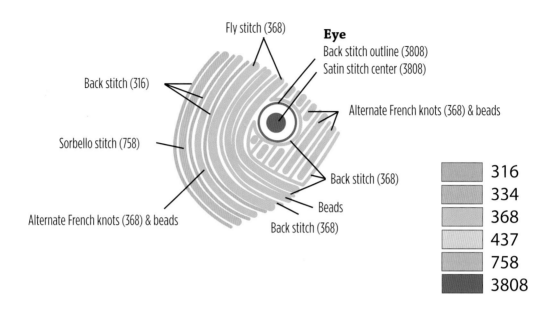

Fly stitch (368)

Eye
Back stitch outline (3808)
Satin stitch center (3808)

Back stitch (316)

Alternate French knots (368) & beads

Sorbello stitch (758)

Back stitch (368)

Beads

Alternate French knots (368) & beads

Back stitch (368)

316
334
368
437
758
3808

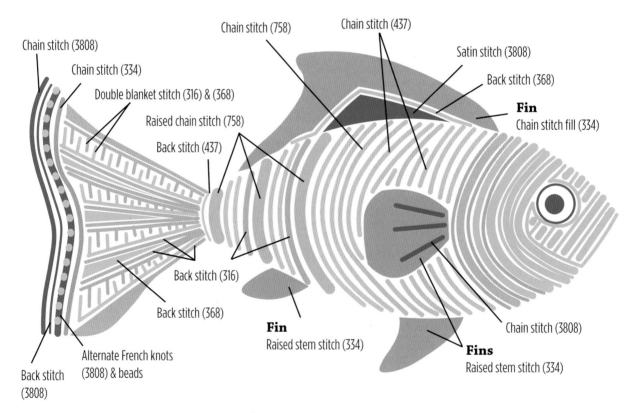

Chain stitch (758)

Chain stitch (437)

Satin stitch (3808)

Chain stitch (3808)

Back stitch (368)

Chain stitch (334)

Fin
Chain stitch fill (334)

Double blanket stitch (316) & (368)

Raised chain stitch (758)

Back stitch (437)

Back stitch (316)

Back stitch (368)

Fin
Raised stem stitch (334)

Alternate French knots (3808) & beads

Chain stitch (3808)

Fins
Raised stem stitch (334)

Back stitch (3808)

Fish
Use six strands of thread for all stitches

1. **Stitch the eyes using DMC 3808.** Use back stitch for the outline, and fill the center part of the eye with satin stitch.

2. **Work the head, starting at the left edge.** Add a row of back stitch using DMC 316, followed by a row of sorbello stitches using DMC 758 and another row of back stitch with DMC 316.

3. **Continue along the head.** Alternate between French knots using DMC 368 and face-up beads for the next row. Follow with another row of back stitch with DMC 316.

4. **Use DMC 368 to make a row of fly stitches.** Add a row of back stitches. Add a full row of beads on their sides. Add another row of back stitch then fly stitch, again with DMC 368.

5. **Finish the head.** Use DMC 368 to make another row of back stitch that is intercepted by the eye. Outline the eye with back stitch using DMC 368. Starting at the right edge, fill the rest of the head with a pattern: rows of back stitch next to rows of French knots that alternate with face-up beads.

6. **Fill the smaller three fins with raised stem stitch using DMC 334.** If desired, gently add stripes of chain stitches using DMC 3808 on top.

7. **Fill the body, starting on the left.** Add a row of back stitch using DMC 437. Follow with this pattern, repeated twice: one row of raised chain stitch using DMC 758, two rows of chain stitch using DMC 437, and two rows of back stitch with DMC 316.

8. **Add another row of raised chain stitch with DMC 758.** Follow with this pattern, repeated twice: three rows of chain stitch with DMC 437, and one row of chain stitch with DMC 758. Fill the remainder of the body with rows of chain stitching using DMC 437. Work around the fin as you fill the body, and use split stitches if needed to fill in any gaps. You may have more rows of chain stitch above the fin than below.

EMBROIDERY TIP

When filling an odd shape with rows of chain stitch, you can begin or end your row with split stitch to taper the thickness of your line. This trick can also be useful when you don't have enough room for another chain, but you have a small gap to fill before the end of the row. You can also add straight stitches as needed to fill in any gaps that catch your eye.

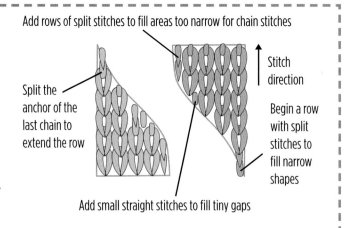

Add rows of split stitches to fill areas too narrow for chain stitches

Stitch direction

Split the anchor of the last chain to extend the row

Begin a row with split stitches to fill narrow shapes

Add small straight stitches to fill tiny gaps

9. Fill the main section of the tail. The top and bottom are filled with back stitch using DMC 316. The rest uses this pattern (from the top): blanket stitch DMC 316, blanket stitch DMC 368, back stitch DMC 316, back stitch fill DMC 368, and back stitch DMC 316. Complete the double blanket stitches first, then use the back stitch and back stitch fill to fill in the spaces between them.

10. Finish the tail with four rows. From right to left: chain stitch with DMC 334, alternating DMC 3808 French knots and face-up beads, back stitch with DMC 3808, and chain stitch with DMC 3808.

11. Fill the bottom shape of the top fin with satin stitch using DMC 3808. Outline along the top with back stitch using DMC 368. For the remainder of the fin, begin with a row of chain stitch using DMC 334 at the right edge of the fin, along the top outline of the shape. Continue to fill with rows following this stitch direction, always starting on the right side of the shape.

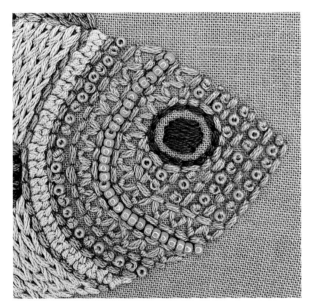

The pattern on the head includes back stitches, sorbello stitches, fly stitches, French knots, and beads. Add or subtract rows to better fit your fish size and stitch style.

To simplify the tail section, skip the double blanket stitch and add more rows of back stitch instead.

Beetle Collection

These bright, colorful beetles are inspired by real insects—with some fun twists! I always love seeing the beetle collections at natural history museums, and I'm always shocked to see the amazing variation in color, size, shape, and texture. It's easy to see why beetles are popular to reproduce with hand embroidery!

Stitch Direction

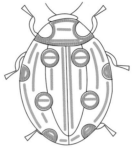

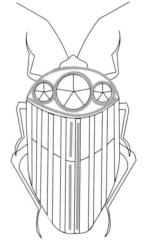
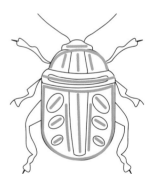

Tips and ideas:

- Each beetle can be its own mini project. Stitch them on four mini embroidery hoops or add them on a jacket or tote.

- If your stitches are getting too crowded, drop down to fewer strands of thread. Have fun using the suggested stitches or substitute with your favorites.

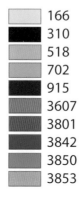

In this project, we intentionally leave gaps in the stitching to allow the fabric color to show through. If you choose to stitch this project on a different color of fabric, you can fill in the gaps with satin stitch using a single strand of white thread.

	166
	310
	518
	702
	915
	3607
	3801
	3842
	3850
	3853

MATERIALS

- 6" (15.2cm) embroidery hoop
- 8" x 8" (20.3 x 20.3cm) white cotton fabric
- Embroidery needles, sizes 6, 9
- Cotton embroidery floss

Beetle 1
Use two strands of thread for all stitches

1. **Outline the head and white eye patches with split stitch using DMC 310.** Fill the head with horizontal satin stitch. Similarly, fill the black spots, first outlining with split stitch and then filling with satin stitch.
2. **Fill the body with back stitch.** Begin with DMC 915 for an initial outline, skipping any place where the black spots meet the body edges. Next use DMC 3801 to make a center vertical line with two rows of back stitch. Continue with this thread, following the 915 curves to fill toward the center. Fill the remaining patches with columns of DMC 3853.
3. **Finish with DMC 310.** Use straight stitch to make antennae and use split stitch to make legs.

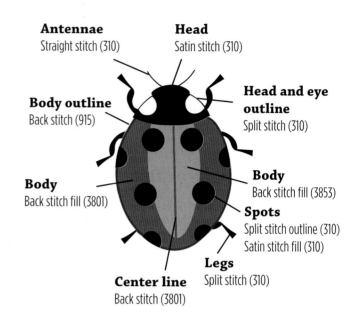

Antennae
Straight stitch (310)

Head
Satin stitch (310)

Body outline
Back stitch (915)

Head and eye outline
Split stitch (310)

Body
Back stitch fill (3801)

Body
Back stitch fill (3853)

Spots
Split stitch outline (310)
Satin stitch fill (310)

Legs
Split stitch (310)

Center line
Back stitch (3801)

Beetle 2
Use two strands of thread unless otherwise noted

1. **Fill the head, excluding the eyes.** Use vertical satin stitch with DMC 702. Fill the eyes with satin stitch using DMC 915. Add a straight stitch beneath each eye using DMC 3801.
2. **Use three strands of DMC 518 to fill the thorax.** Make vertical rows of chain stitch. Continue with this thread, using it to outline and fill the legs with split stitch.
3. **Use DMC 3842 to outline the thorax with split stitch.** Continue with this thread, adding straight stitches under the first segment of each leg. Create the antennae using whipped back stitch.
4. **Fill the thick pink stripes on the bottom body.** Use split stitch with DMC 3607. Outline each stripe first and then fill. Use three strands of DMC 518 to outline the white stripes (negative space) with split stitch.
5. **Finish with three strands of DMC 166.** Make vertical chain stitch stripes on the body and French knot dots on the thorax. Some of these guidelines may be hidden by previous stitching, so use your best judgment for placement.

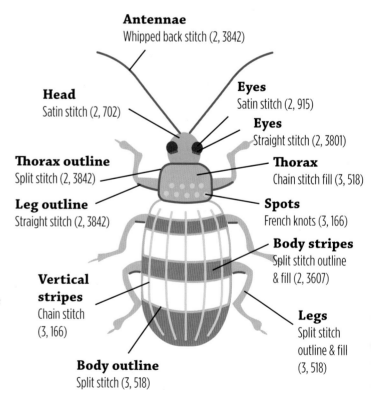

Antennae
Whipped back stitch (2, 3842)

Head
Satin stitch (2, 702)

Eyes
Satin stitch (2, 915)

Eyes
Straight stitch (2, 3801)

Thorax outline
Split stitch (2, 3842)

Thorax
Chain stitch fill (3, 518)

Leg outline
Straight stitch (2, 3842)

Spots
French knots (3, 166)

Body stripes
Split stitch outline & fill (2, 3607)

Vertical stripes
Chain stitch (3, 166)

Legs
Split stitch outline & fill (3, 518)

Body outline
Split stitch (3, 518)

Beetle 3

Use three strands of thread unless otherwise noted

1. **Use six strands of DMC 3607 for the woven wheel roses.** Fill the thorax shape with back stitch using DMC 915. Outline the shape and the roses first, then fill.

2. **Make the long vertical stripes on the body.** Use DMC 3842 for columns of stem stitch. Fill the spaces between with stem stitch, using DMC 3853 at the top and DMC 3850 at the bottom.

3. **Outline and fill the head and legs.** Use two strands of DMC 3801 with split stitch. Use split stitch to create the antennae. Finish by making the French knot eyes with two strands of DMC 702.

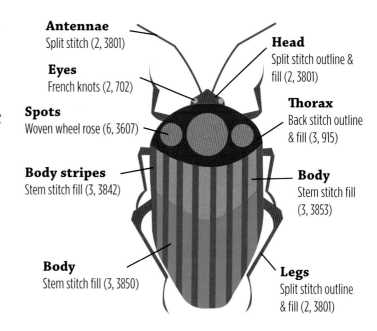

Antennae
Split stitch (2, 3801)

Head
Split stitch outline & fill (2, 3801)

Eyes
French knots (2, 702)

Thorax
Back stitch outline & fill (3, 915)

Spots
Woven wheel rose (6, 3607)

Body stripes
Stem stitch fill (3, 3842)

Body
Stem stitch fill (3, 3853)

Body
Stem stitch fill (3, 3850)

Legs
Split stitch outline & fill (2, 3801)

Beetle 4

Use two strands of thread for all stitches

1. **Use DMC 915 to create the padded satin stitch spots on the body.** For the long spot on the middle section, switch to split stitch to fill. Outline all of these spots with split stitch using DMC 310.

2. **Use DMC 3850 to outline the body segments with split stitch.** Pay attention to the diagram. Begin to fill the body with split stitch using DMC 702. Use a vertical stitch direction when possible, but modify around the spots to more easily fill the space. Finish filling the center body stripe with DMC 166 using split stitch.

3. **Use DMC 310 to outline the legs with split stitch.** Create the antennae with back stitch. Finish with DMC 3853, using it to fill the legs with split stitch and to create the French knot eyes.

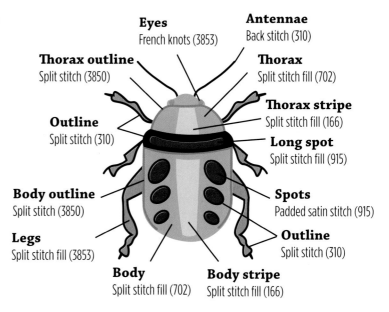

Eyes
French knots (3853)

Antennae
Back stitch (310)

Thorax outline
Split stitch (3850)

Thorax
Split stitch fill (702)

Thorax stripe
Split stitch fill (166)

Outline
Split stitch (310)

Long spot
Split stitch fill (915)

Body outline
Split stitch (3850)

Spots
Padded satin stitch (915)

Legs
Split stitch fill (3853)

Outline
Split stitch (310)

Body
Split stitch fill (702)

Body stripe
Split stitch fill (166)

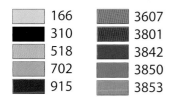

166	3607
310	3801
518	3842
702	3850
915	3853

You don't have to be a fan of
real bugs to enjoy this project.

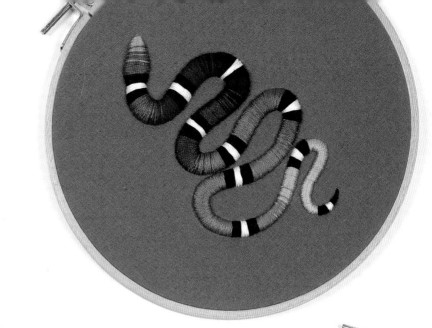

Chapter 7

Confident Beginner Creatures

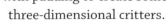

Push beginner embroidery stitches further with these more complicated animal designs. These projects require a bit more patience and precision, and they give you an opportunity to play with padding to create some very three-dimensional critters.

Striped Gecko

Lizards and geckos come in so many fun colors, shapes, and sizes! For this project, I picked some variegated threads and used wool padding to create a dynamic, three-dimensional gecko. In the future, I plan to create a collection of geckos, using more colors and resizing the pattern to frame them in different hoop sizes.

Tips and ideas:

- I used two variegated thread colors from COSMO to create the dynamic stripes on the gecko. This project would be fun with other variegated thread colors too. I suggest finding threads that share similar colors but are different enough that you can distinguish between them.

- If you are looking for similar solid colors of thread from DMC, I suggest 14, 3846, 3755, and 3811 for Seasons 9003; and 798, 3810, 156, and 3746 for Seasons 8056.

- It's okay to use the variegated thread without worrying about matching the color pattern between cut lengths of floss. If you do want a more regular color transition, pay attention to the color pattern so you can match up lengths of thread.

- If you are having trouble sourcing padding or struggling to use it, the pattern can be worked without. You can also use felt instead, using the pattern to cut a piece to match the head, body, and tail of the gecko. Alternatively, you can also pad the body with bulky stitches like chain stitch, using six strands of any color thread to build up a base to be covered with your satin stitches.

The completed gecko, as seen from the side, highlights the three-dimensionality created with the padding.

MATERIALS

- 6" (15.2cm) embroidery hoop
- 8" x 8" (20.3 x 20.3cm) white cotton fabric
- Embroidery needles, sizes 6, 9
- Wool cotton padding
- Cotton embroidery floss

991
Seasons 8056
Seasons 9003

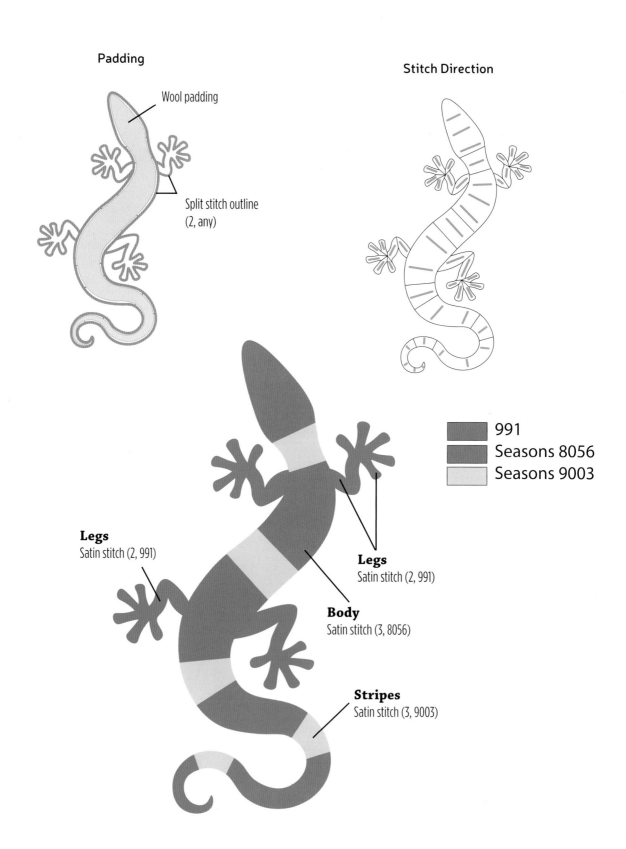

Padding

Wool padding

Split stitch outline
(2, any)

Stitch Direction

991
Seasons 8056
Seasons 9003

Legs
Satin stitch (2, 991)

Legs
Satin stitch (2, 991)

Body
Satin stitch (3, 8056)

Stripes
Satin stitch (3, 9003)

Gecko

1. Outline the gecko with split stitch. Use two strands of any color thread. This outline will be covered with your satin stitches, and it helps to maintain a smooth shape. Because the padding will cover the guidelines for the stripes, you may want to make small, straight stitch marks using a different color along this outline to guide you in the next steps.

2. Select a length of wool padding. Mold to roughly the shape of the gecko, excluding the legs. Begin to anchor it to the fabric, using a single strand of any color to strap down the padding within the split stitch outline. Use gentle tension to avoid making any noticeable dents in the padding, making as many stitches as desired to shape it.

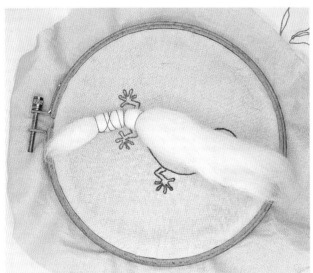

3. Continue forming the padding on the head. Make the anchoring stitches at different angles to help define the shape of the padding. Add extra stitches near the neck to help compress the padding within the guidelines. As the head shape narrows, use scissors to remove some of the thickness of the padding, sculpting a tapered shape and trimming away any excess length.

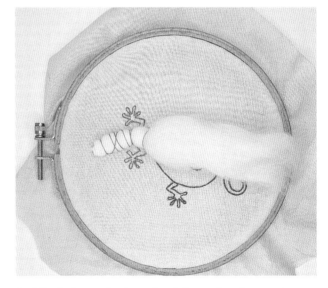

4. Work down the length of the gecko. Secure the padding with more anchoring stitches. If needed, add more strips of wool to increase the thickness of the body. As the tail narrows, begin to thin out the padding by cutting it away. Secure the padding from head to tail.

5. Use three strands of thread to begin covering the tail. Use satin stitch with Seasons 8056. Be mindful of the tension, using care to avoid collapsing the padding.

6. Continue to cover the padding with satin stitch. Switch to Seasons 9003 for the stripes. Choose to make five stripes as shown in the diagram, or make as many as you like.

7. Pad the toe pads and upper legs. Use six strands of any thread with straight stitches. Use two strands of DMC 991 to fill the legs with satin stitch, beginning with the toes. See the diagram for suggested stitch direction.

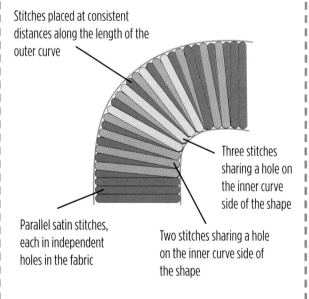

Stitches placed at consistent distances along the length of the outer curve

Three stitches sharing a hole on the inner curve side of the shape

Parallel satin stitches, each in independent holes in the fabric

Two stitches sharing a hole on the inner curve side of the shape

EMBROIDERY TIP

While filling the gecko with satin stitch, the stitch direction needs to change with the curves of the body and tail. Some of the stitches will need to share the same hole in the fabric on the shortened side of the shape to compensate for the curve.

By using variegated thread, we create a uniquely striped gecko. If you prefer a more consistent look, use solid-colored thread.

Rainbow Snake

I used to catch garter snakes when I was young. I was fascinated by their curves, stripes, and quick flicking tongues. Today, I run from snake encounters, but I still think that they are beautiful animals! For this design, I took some liberties to create a snake with an eye-catching rainbow body and black-and-white stripes. To really make a dynamic rendition, I used wool padding to make this serpent three-dimensional.

Padding

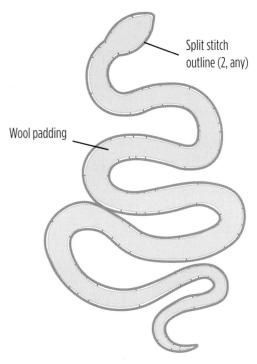

Split stitch outline (2, any)

Wool padding

Tips and ideas:

- It's okay to skip the wool filling! The design is still amazing when stitched straight onto your fabric without the padding. Or you can use a bulky chain stitch with six strands of thread to create a base of padding. You can also choose a different color palette, such as a transition from a dark to a light green, or maybe add some metallic or iridescent threads.

Stitch Direction

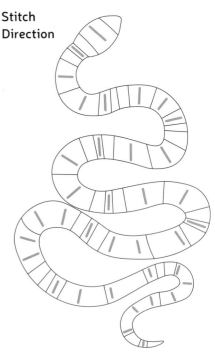

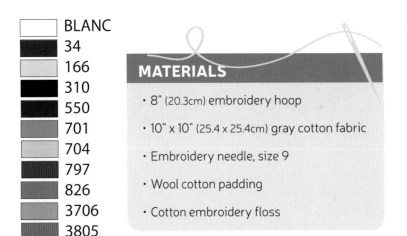

	BLANC
	34
	166
	310
	550
	701
	704
	797
	826
	3706
	3805
	3809
	3814

MATERIALS

- 8" (20.3cm) embroidery hoop
- 10" x 10" (25.4 x 25.4cm) gray cotton fabric
- Embroidery needle, size 9
- Wool cotton padding
- Cotton embroidery floss

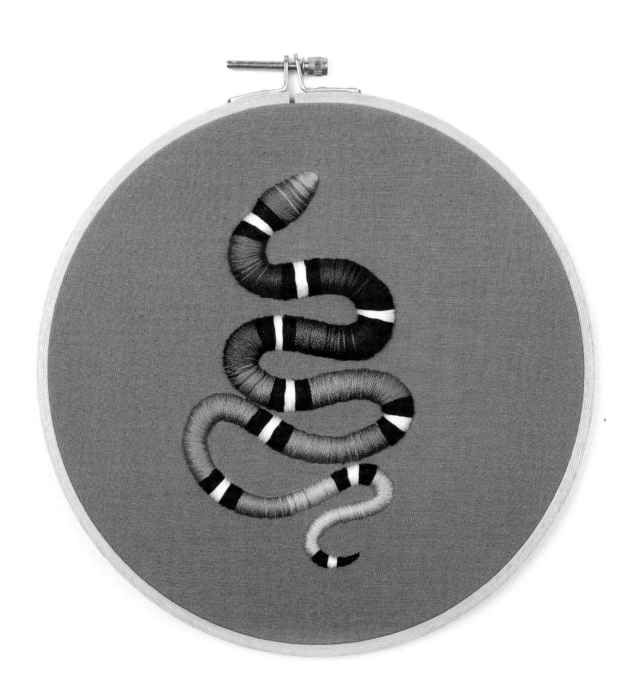

Snake

1. **Outline the snake with split stitch.** Use two strands of any color thread. This outline will be covered with your satin stitches, and it helps to maintain a smooth shape. Because the padding will cover the color transition guidelines, you may want to make small, straight stitch marks using a different color along this outline to guide you in future steps.

2. **Roll small clumps of cotton between your palms.** Make an assortment of strips 4"–10" (10.2–25.4cm) in length. Beginning at the tail, start forming the body while using the snake outline as a template. Add more strips of wool to increase the thickness of the body.

3. **Anchor down the wool along the guidelines.** Use a single strand of any color thread and gentle tension to avoid making any noticeable dents in the padding. Add additional wool strips as needed to create the body form.

4. **Form the head of the snake.** Anchor down the form and cut or pull away any excess wool lengths.

5. **Begin covering the tail with satin stitch.** Use two strands of DMC 310. Be mindful of the tension, using care to avoid collapsing the padding, and be sure to cover the original split stitch outline. Switch to DMC BLANC and then back to DMC 310 where indicated on the diagram.

6. **Switch to two strands of DMC 166.** Continue to cover the split stitch outline and padding with satin stitch. Blend into the next color (DMC 704) by slowly adding a few stitches of this new color within the DMC 166 satin stitch.

7. **Continue to cover the padding with satin stitch.** Refer to the diagram for suggested color placement. Adjust the stitch direction as described on page 88 when you encounter curves.

The padding is anchored and shaped by the initial stitches. Pull out or cut away the padding at either end to help shape the tapered head and tail.

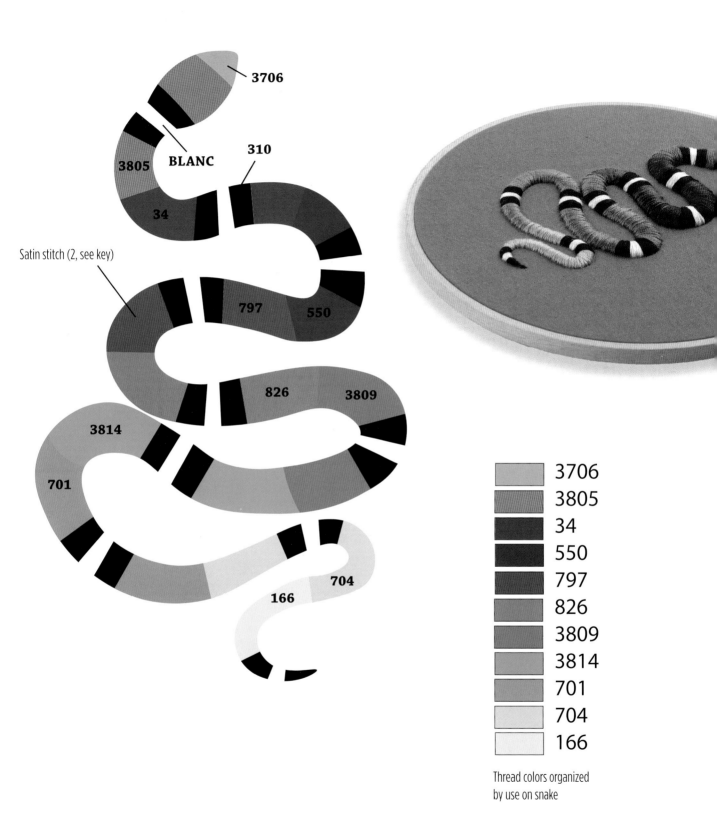

3706

BLANC

310

3805

34

Satin stitch (2, see key)

797

550

826

3809

3814

701

3814

701

166

704

3706
3805
34
550
797
826
3809
3814
701
704
166

Thread colors organized
by use on snake

Rainbow Snake 93

Wild Fern Deer

My first book, *Animal Embroidery Workbook*, included a pattern featuring a sweet fawn in a field of wildflowers. That little fawn has grown up! This deer is similarly stitched using back stitch, but he is nestled within a patch of thick, green ferns.

Tips and ideas:

- Use care when stitching the deer, referring to the color diagram regularly and making sure you are using the correct brown hue. You can also stitch the deer with long and short stitch, using the same color and stitch direction diagrams as a guide.

- The front and middle rows of ferns can be a bit tricky to create, as their guidelines will be covered by the back row. Use your best judgment when creating these plants. Remember that all ferns in nature are different, so it is okay if yours do not look identical to those in the sample hoop!

Stitch Direction

MATERIALS

- 4" (10.2cm) embroidery hoop

- 6" x 6" (15.2 x 15.2cm) sky blue cotton fabric

- Embroidery needles, sizes 3, 9

- Cotton embroidery floss

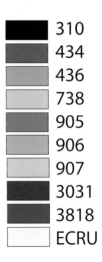

■	310
■	434
■	436
■	738
■	905
■	906
■	907
■	3031
■	3818
□	ECRU

Deer

Use two strands of thread for all stitches

1. Use DMC 310 to outline the eyes with back stitch. Fill with satin stitch, covering the back stitch. In a similar manner, fill the nose. Add straight stitch eye highlights over the satin stitch with ECRU.

2. Outline around the eyes with back stitch. Start with one outline using ECRU and then another using DMC 738. Outline the nose with ECRU only.

3. Outline the top of the head. Fill down to the nose with back stitch rows of DMC 434. Fill the rest of the head with DMC 436, outlining the remaining space first and then filling with back stitch.

4. Fill the ears. Start at the top with DMC 3031 using back stitch. Work the inside of the ears with ECRU, DMC 738, and DMC 434 as shown in the diagram.

5. Use rows of back stitch to fill the neck. Transition from ECRU at the center to DMC 738

through DMC 436 and DMC 434 at the edge. Fill the back with back stitch using DMC 434.

6. Outline and fill the antlers with back stitch. Outline the shadow sides of the antlers with DMC 436 and the upper highlighted sides with ECRU. Fill the remaining space with DMC 738.

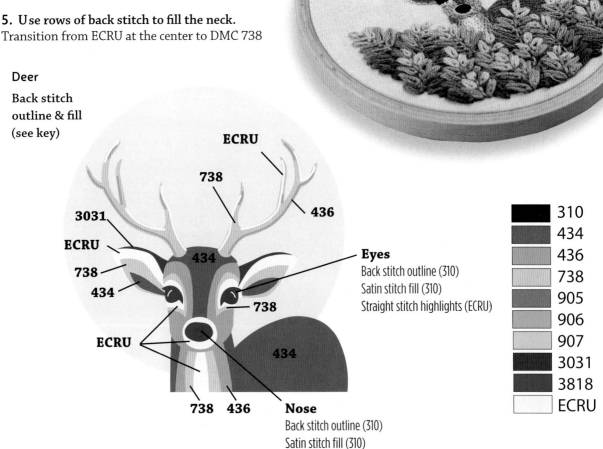

Deer

Back stitch outline & fill (see key)

ECRU
738
436
3031
ECRU
738
434
434
738
ECRU
738   436
434

Eyes
Back stitch outline (310)
Satin stitch fill (310)
Straight stitch highlights (ECRU)

Nose
Back stitch outline (310)
Satin stitch fill (310)

■	310
■	434
■	436
■	738
■	905
■	906
■	907
■	3031
■	3818
□	ECRU

Ferns

1. Create each fern frond. Back stitch a stem using two strands of DMC 906. Create the detached chain stitch fronds using six strands of green thread: begin at the tip of the fern with DMC 907, then work down the sides of the fern, transitioning through DMC 906, 905, and 3818 as illustrated in the diagram.

2. Stitch the back row of ferns first. Complete these ferns through the final dark green (DMC 3818) fronds, creating a total of 15 fronds per fern.

3. Work the middle row, overlapping the back row. Some guidelines will be covered by the front row, so refer to the diagram to guide you. Work the middle row down to the bottom edge of your design; some of these ferns will extend to the dark green fronds while others will stop at a lighter green. Just focus on filling the space to the edge of the design.

4. Finish by creating the front row of ferns. This row will be cropped after or within the DMC 906 fronds. Add more ferns if needed to cover any spots where the fabric shows through.

It's important to closely follow the color key and stitch direction diagram when filling the deer with tiny back stitches. Enlarge the design to make the project easier. Switch to thread painting using a single strand of thread for a challenge!

907

906

905

3818

Fern fronds
Detached chain stitch leaves (6, see key)

Stem
Back stitch (2, 906)

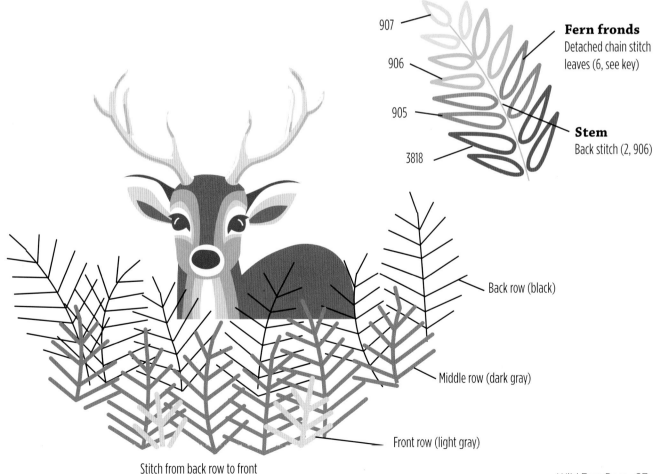

Back row (black)

Middle row (dark gray)

Front row (light gray)

Stitch from back row to front

Bumblebee Bouquet

We are so lucky to share this planet with bees! This floral wreath features some bee favorites: coneflowers, marigolds, zinnias, black-eyed Susans, and cosmos. This project provides a fun opportunity to play with bright colors and an interesting mix of textures. The leaves and larger flowers sit low to the fabric while the remaining flowers use bulky stitches. The stars of the show, our bumblebees, are created with a tightly cut Turkey work, resulting in an amazingly fuzzy texture.

Creating stripes of color in a block of Turkey work can be challenging. Some of my bees have perfect stripes and others do not. If you are having trouble with the Turkey work or if you prefer your bees to look more uniform, you can use padded satin stitch for the bee bodies instead.

Tips and ideas:

- I used a variegated green thread from COSMO for the leaves, but you can substitute with another rich variegated green. If you need to use a solid color from DMC, I suggest 987, 561, or 3345.

- The shapes in the design overlap each other, and there are many options for which elements could be stitched first. Sometimes it can be easier to stitch foreground flowers first, but not always and not for everyone.

- Use the suggested instructions below as a guide, but remain flexible as you work through the project. Explore the options and see what works best for you.

- Enlarge the project if you find the details too small at the current size.

- Add additional leaves and small French knot flowers throughout your project to add more color and to cover any mistakes.

	BLANC
	33
	210
	310
	304
	351
	720
	726
	744
	902
	922
	972
	3371
	3820
	Seasons 8024

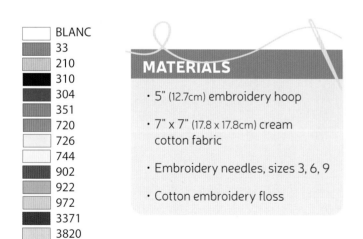

MATERIALS

- 5" (12.7cm) embroidery hoop

- 7" x 7" (17.8 x 17.8cm) cream cotton fabric

- Embroidery needles, sizes 3, 6, 9

- Cotton embroidery floss

Wreath and Bees

1. Make the zinnias. Use satin stitch with six strands of DMC 972 to fill the centers. Make the petals out of detached chain stitches using six strands of the designated color, according to the diagram. Create the petals near the center first, then fill in the gaps in the second row.

2. Make the marigolds. Use six strands of thread, following the colors suggested in the diagram. Begin with a central French knot, then surround it with a circle of six more French knots. Use fly stitch for the remaining petals, offset from the previous row, making as many rows as needed to fill the guidelines.

3. Make the red coneflowers. Use six strands of DMC 902 to start filling the flower center with French knots. Switch to DMC 3371 for the French knots closer to the petals. Use two strands of DMC 304 to fill the petals with satin stitch. Finish by adding straight stitches on top of the petals using three strand of DMC 902.

4. Make the black-eyed Susan. Use six strands of DMC 3371 to fill the center with padded satin stitch. Use one strand of DMC 972 to fill the petals with satin stitch.

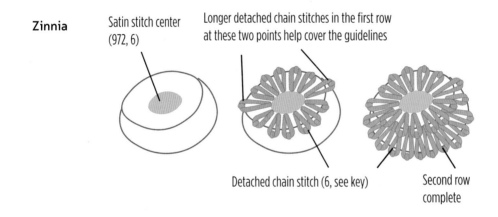

Zinnia

Satin stitch center (972, 6)

Longer detached chain stitches in the first row at these two points help cover the guidelines

Detached chain stitch (6, see key)

Second row complete

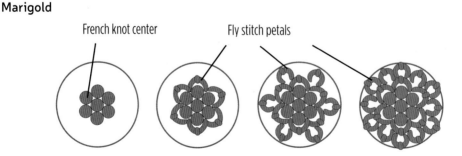

Marigold

French knot center

Fly stitch petals

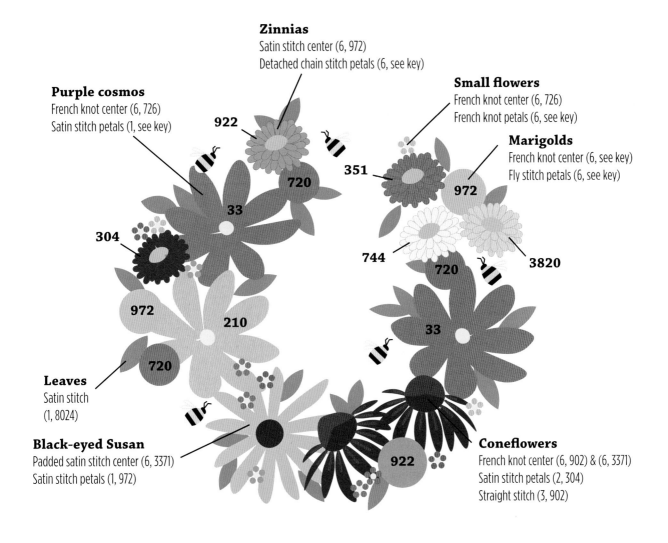

Zinnias
Satin stitch center (6, 972)
Detached chain stitch petals (6, see key)

Small flowers
French knot center (6, 726)
French knot petals (6, see key)

Marigolds
French knot center (6, see key)
Fly stitch petals (6, see key)

Purple cosmos
French knot center (6, 726)
Satin stitch petals (1, see key)

Leaves
Satin stitch
(1, 8024)

Black-eyed Susan
Padded satin stitch center (6, 3371)
Satin stitch petals (1, 972)

Coneflowers
French knot center (6, 902) & (6, 3371)
Satin stitch petals (2, 304)
Straight stitch (3, 902)

922
351
972
744
720
3820
304
33
972
210
720
33
922

Bumblebee

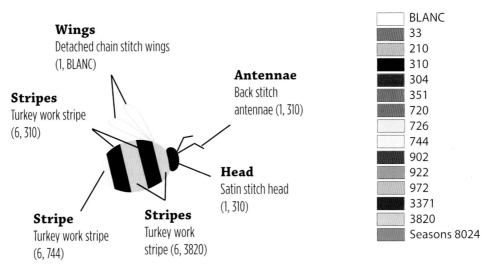

Wings
Detached chain stitch wings
(1, BLANC)

Antennae
Back stitch
antennae (1, 310)

Stripes
Turkey work stripe
(6, 310)

Head
Satin stitch head
(1, 310)

Stripe
Turkey work stripe
(6, 744)

Stripes
Turkey work
stripe (6, 3820)

	BLANC
	33
	210
	310
	304
	351
	720
	726
	744
	902
	922
	972
	3371
	3820
	Seasons 8024

5. Make the purple cosmos. Fill the centers with French knots using six strands of DMC 726. Fill the petals with satin stitch using a single strand of DMC 33 or DMC 210, as shown in the diagram.

6. Make the leaves. Use a single strand of Seasons 8024 to fill the leaves with satin stitch. Add more leaves if desired.

7. Make the small flowers. Use French knots with six strands of thread. Use DMC 726 for the centers and either a purple or orange color thread for the petals. See the diagram for suggested color placement.

8. Create the bee bodies. Fill the shape with five rows of Turkey work stitch. Use six strands of thread, beginning near the head with a row of DMC 3820. Complete the rows according to the diagram, using DMC 310 and DMC 744 before tightly trimming the Turkey work stitches.

9. Create the bee heads. Use a single strand of DMC 310 with satin stitch. Create the antennae using back stitch. Create the wings out of two detached chain stitches using one strand of DMC BLANC.

I love the textural contrast of the flat, satin stitched flowers and leaves next to the dimensional florals and bees.

Forest Elk

I only recently learned about larches, the deciduous conifer trees that turn an amazing bright yellow in the fall. My friend's photos while hiking the Enchantments in Washington state inspired me to recreate them with hand embroidery. I decided to frame the landscape within the shape of an elk, one of my favorite forest animals. Have fun recreating these natural textures using satin stitch, split stitch, fishbone stitch, straight stitch, and French knots.

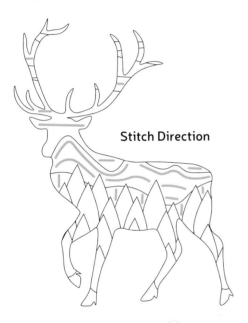

Stitch Direction

Tips and ideas:
- The antlers are challenging to fill, which is why this project is placed in this chapter. Go slow and take your time. Sketch in horizontal lines on your fabric to help keep your stitches straight. If you are finding the pattern too difficult at its current size, please enlarge it.

- Be a little messy when creating the trees. Each straight stitch is a tree branch. Exaggerate these stitches over the background stitches, and create variety in length and angle.

- The stitch direction of the trees within the skinny leg shapes may devolve. Use your best judgment to fill these sections with overlapping, angled straight stitches. We are trying to recreate natural tree branches, so these stitches will not be uniform. Let them be wild, concentrating only on staying within the shape of the elk.

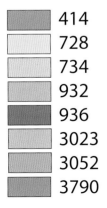

414
728
734
932
936
3023
3052
3790

MATERIALS

- 6" (15.2cm) embroidery hoop

- 8" x 8" (20.3 x 20.3cm) light gray cotton fabric

- Embroidery needle, size 9

- Cotton embroidery floss

Elk

1. **Use a single strand of thread to fill the sky.** Use horizontal satin stitch, switching to split stitch if needed to fill across larger sections. Use DMC 414 for the gray clouds and DMC 932 for the blue sky.

2. **Fill the distant mountains.** Use split stitch with two strands of DMC 3023. Outline along the upper edge first, then echo this stitch direction as you continue making rows to fill the shape. Avoid stitching completely over the tree guidelines so you can still see them. Alternatively, choose to stitch over them and improvise the location of the trees in the later steps.

3. **Fill the brown hills.** Use two strands of DMC 3790 with vertical split stitch.

4. **Create the trees from back to front.** Use three strands of thread and begin each tree with a base of fishbone stitch. Add additional straight stitches at the center of the shape, then fill with angled straight stitches. See the color key for suggested thread color placement.

5. **Finish by filling the bottom section.** Use French knots with two strands of DMC 3790. Outline the shape with knots first to help define the shape, then fill.

EMBROIDERY TIP

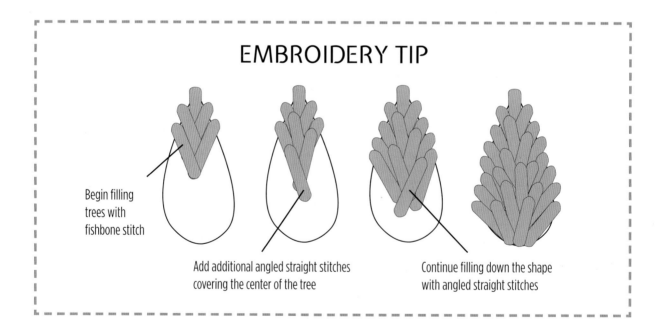

Begin filling trees with fishbone stitch

Add additional angled straight stitches covering the center of the tree

Continue filling down the shape with angled straight stitches

The skinny antlers and legs of the elk can be challenging to fill. Take your time and be sure to use a good light source while stitching.

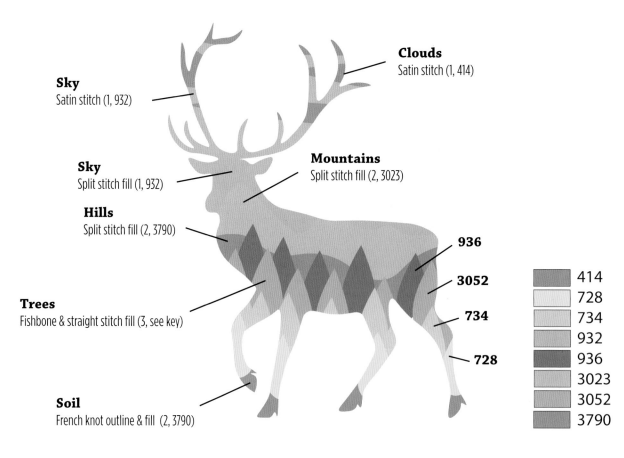

Sky
Satin stitch (1, 932)

Clouds
Satin stitch (1, 414)

Sky
Split stitch fill (1, 932)

Mountains
Split stitch fill (2, 3023)

Hills
Split stitch fill (2, 3790)

Trees
Fishbone & straight stitch fill (3, see key)

Soil
French knot outline & fill (2, 3790)

936

3052

734

728

	414
	728
	734
	932
	936
	3023
	3052
	3790

Mountain Bear

The idea of filling a bear shape with a mountain landscape is not new, but I think I've included some unique textures and stitches in this rendition. The sky and mountains are filled with the same stitch, but by using different colors, numbers of threads, and stitch direction, we create interesting variation in the background of our landscape.

Stitch Direction

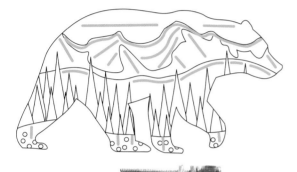

Tips and ideas:

- If the wheatear fill trees are too challenging, use straight stitches to fill the trees like in Forest Elk (page 103). The guidelines for the second row of trees will be covered by the first row of trees. Use your best judgment to improvise their locations.

- Many of the trees are cropped, so you will need to edit and adapt the wheatear stitch to some irregular shapes; do your best and use straight stitches to fill in any gaps.

Beads can add a special sparkle and texture to your embroidery work. Substitute with French or colonial knots if you do not have any.

MATERIALS

- 5" (12.7cm) embroidery hoop

- 7" x 7" (17.8 x 17.8cm) light blue-green cotton fabric

- Embroidery needles, sizes 3, 9

- Beading needle

- Transparent-rainbow frosted ruby beads, round size 11/0

- Thread for beads in a matching color, such as DMC 917

- Cotton embroidery floss

	BLANC
	518
	704
	794
	988
	3345
	3363

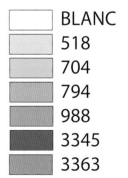

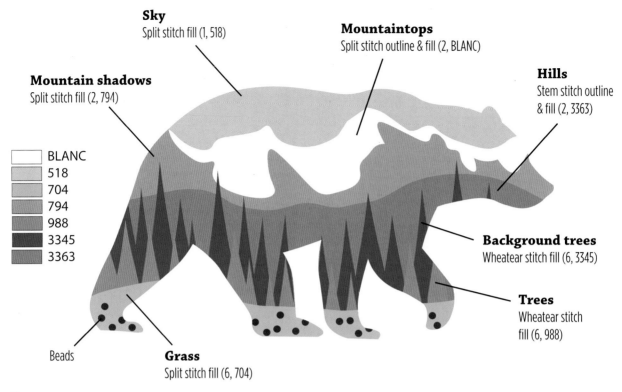

Sky
Split stitch fill (1, 518)

Mountaintops
Split stitch outline & fill (2, BLANC)

Hills
Stem stitch outline
& fill (2, 3363)

Mountain shadows
Split stitch fill (2, 794)

BLANC
518
704
794
988
3345
3363

Background trees
Wheatear stitch fill (6, 3345)

Trees
Wheatear stitch
fill (6, 988)

Beads

Grass
Split stitch fill (6, 704)

Bear

1. Make the sky. Fill with horizontal split stitch using one strand of DMC 518.

2. Fill the top section of the mountains. Use split stitch with two strands of BLANC. Outline the top edge first, then continue making split stitch rows to fill the space while echoing the stitch direction of the first row.

3. Fill the shadow sides of the mountain range. Use two strands of DMC 794 with split stitch and a diagonal stitch direction.

4. Fill the green hills. Use stem stitch with two strands of DMC 3363. Begin with the top outline, then fill down the shape by row. Choose to leave gaps, leaving the tree guidelines visible, or chose to cover them, using your best judgment for tree placement in the next step.

5. Create the trees using wheatear stitch. Make the straight stitch branches as long or short as desired. Use six strands of green thread, making the background trees with the darker DMC 3345 and the foreground trees with DMC 988.

6. Make the bright flowers. Attach beads on their sides to the paws. Alternatively, make these flowers out of French or colonial knots using six strands of a pink thread, such as DMC 915.

7. Finish with the grass. Use six strands of DMC 704 to fill the remaining space on the paws with split stitch.

Ringtail

Ringtails are related to raccoons, and they live in North American deserts. These animals have very interesting marks on their faces, and of course they sport a long, striped tail. Since we are already stitching a raccoon using long and short stitch later in this book, I decided to use textural stitches and felt padding to recreate this critter.

Padding

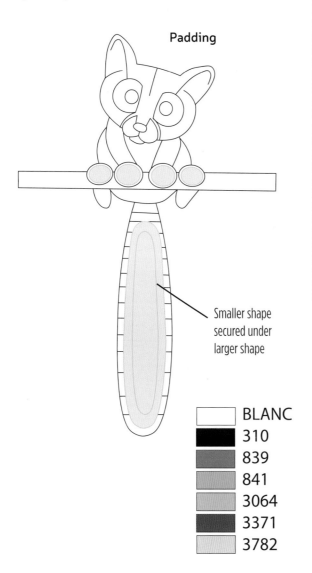

Smaller shape secured under larger shape

⬜	BLANC
⬛	310
▩	839
▨	841
▨	3064
▩	3371
▨	3782

Tips and ideas:

- The directions assume that you are stitching the project at the exact same size with the same thread thickness and the same stitch tension as me. You may need to make adjustments while stitching the face, such as changing the number of threads you are using, swapping between chain and split stitch, or adding extra rows.

- To show off that fluffy tail, we will be using chain stitch on top of a padded base. Unfortunately, when filling a shape with chain stitch, some of the fabric can show through between rows and through the center of each chain. I chose to cover the padding on the tail first with satin stitch, to both hide the felt and to add extra padding.

MATERIALS

- 5" x 8" (12.7 x 20.3cm) embroidery hoop

- 7" x 10" (17.8 x 25.4cm) dark blue cotton fabric

- 5" x 5" (12.7 x 12.7cm) felt fabric

- Fabric scissors

- Embroidery needles, sizes 3, 6, 9

- Cotton embroidery floss

Eyes
Satin stitch (3, 310)
Straight stitch highlight (1, BLANC)
Split stitch highlight (1, BLANC)

Chain stitch (6, 3371)

Chain stitch (6, BLANC)

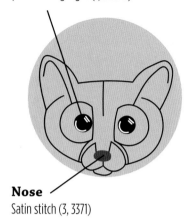

Nose
Satin stitch (3, 3371)

Split stitch (6, 3371)

Satin stitch (3, BLANC)

Back stitch (6, 3782)

Satin stitch (2, 3064)

Chain stitch (6, 839)

Split stitch (6, 839)

Chain stitch (6, 3782)

Whiskers
Straight stitch (1, 310)

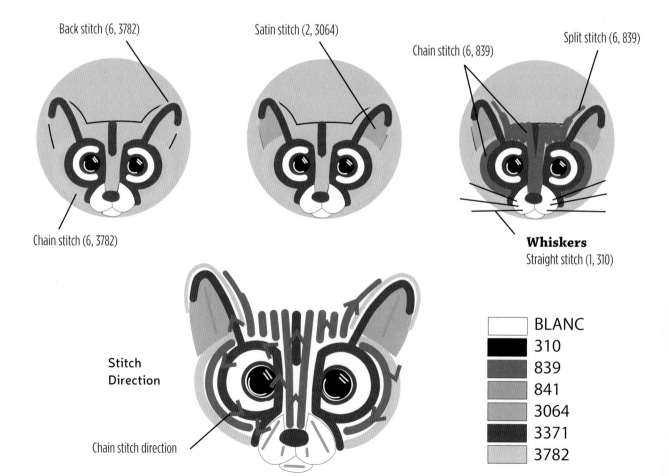

Stitch
Direction

Chain stitch direction

	BLANC
	310
	839
	841
	3064
	3371
	3782

Head

1. Carefully cut out the paw and tail pieces from the felt. Attach them to the main fabric with small straight stitches. Secure the small tail piece first, then cover with the large tail piece.

2. Fill the eyes and nose. Use satin stitch and three strands of thread, with DMC 310 for the eyes and DMC 3371 for the nose. Use one strand of BLANC to add straight stitch highlights on top of the eye. Add a short length of split stitch that partially lines the left corners of the eyes.

3. Outline the eyes. Use split stitch with six strands of DMC 3371. Switch to chain stitch to make the dark markings on the face, following the diagram for suggested stitch direction.

4. Fill the white spaces near the eyes. Use six strands of BLANC with a row of chain stitch. Use three strands of BLANC to fill the areas near the mouth with satin stitch.

5. Create the tan highlights on the ears. Use back stitch with six strands of DMC 3782. Switch to chain stitch to make a row of tan fur on both sides of the face, starting near the ears and working toward the muzzle.

6. Fill the insides of the ears with satin stitch. Keep a vertical stitch direction and use two strands of DMC 3064.

7. Fill the rest of the head with chain stitch. Use six strands of DMC 839, referring to the diagram for suggested stitch direction. Transition from chain stitch to a couple of split stitches to taper the row that touches each ear. Use a single strand of DMC 310 to make straight stitch whiskers.

For consistency, I decided to fill the tail with rows of chain stitch so that it matches the texture on the ringtail's face.

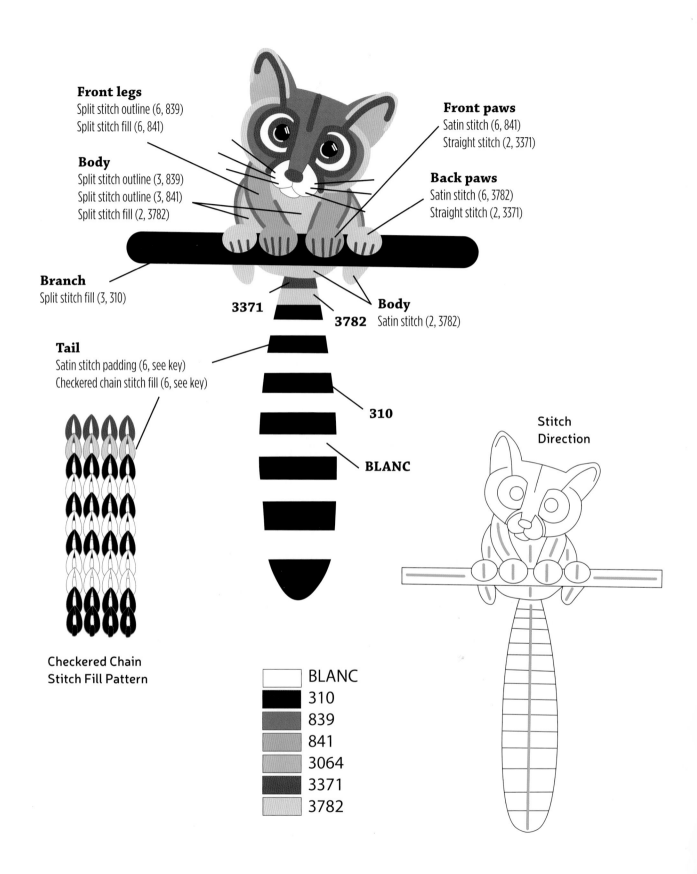

Front legs
Split stitch outline (6, 839)
Split stitch fill (6, 841)

Body
Split stitch outline (3, 839)
Split stitch outline (3, 841)
Split stitch fill (2, 3782)

Front paws
Satin stitch (6, 841)
Straight stitch (2, 3371)

Back paws
Satin stitch (6, 3782)
Straight stitch (2, 3371)

Branch
Split stitch fill (3, 310)

3371

3782

Body
Satin stitch (2, 3782)

Tail
Satin stitch padding (6, see key)
Checkered chain stitch fill (6, see key)

310

BLANC

Checkered Chain
Stitch Fill Pattern

Stitch
Direction

	BLANC
	310
	839
	841
	3064
	3371
	3782

Body and Tail

1. **Fill the branch.** Use three strands of DMC 310 with split stitch, using a horizontal stitch direction.

2. **Fill the paws.** Use satin stitch with six strands of thread, completely covering the felt. Use DMC 841 for the front paws and DMC 3782 for the back paws. Make straight stitches on top of the paws with two strands of DMC 3371, using gentle tension to avoid compressing the padding.

3. **Outline the front legs.** Use split stitch with six strands of DMC 839, as illustrated in the diagram. Fill the legs with split stitch using six strands of DMC 841.

4. **Outline the body with split stitch.** First use three strands of DMC 839, then use three strands of DMC 841. Fill the remainder of the body above the branch using vertical split stitch with two strands of DMC 3782. Switch to satin stitch to fill the body parts below the branch, including the bottoms of the back paws.

5. **Cover the felt on the tail.** Use horizontal satin stitch with six strands of thread, switching between DMC 310 and BLANC to make the black and white stripes. Use DMC 3371 and DMC 3782 for the two stripes closest to the body. This layer covers the felt and adds more padding to the tail.

6. **Fill the tail with checkered chain stitch.** Use six strands of thread and begin the first column at the base of the tail where it meets the body. Start with a stripe each of DMC 3371 and DMC 3782 before alternating between DMC 310 and BLANC down the length of the tail. Each stripe is one to two chains before switching colors.

EMBROIDERY TIP

Switching between the thread colors to create the horizontal tail stripes can be awkward and tedious. I added columns of split stitch between my columns of chain stitch to speed up the filling process. The resulting texture is very similar to chain stitch, and you may decide to substitute the split stitch for chain stitch to cover the entire tail. Another option is to use slightly overlapping detached chain stitches to mimic a solid chain of alternating thread colors.

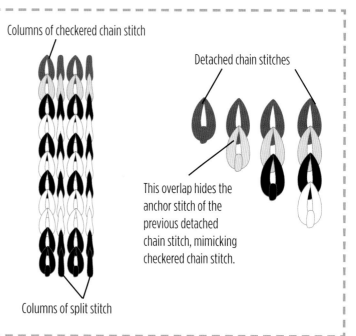

Columns of checkered chain stitch

Detached chain stitches

This overlap hides the anchor stitch of the previous detached chain stitch, mimicking checkered chain stitch.

Columns of split stitch

Chapter 8

Beginner Thread Painting Critters

Explore beginner thread painting and wire slip construction in this next section of animal designs. We will get opportunities to use long and short stitch to fill leaves, flower petals, feathers, and more!

Penguin Family

This is our first opportunity to play with long and short stitch, and we are using it to recreate the soft color transition on the necks of two emperor penguins. I love that splash of yellow on their necks and chests as well as the stark contrast it creates against the black-and-white feathers. Young penguins look very different from their parents, so have fun with Turkey work to make those wild, fluffy feathers.

Tips and ideas:

- The floral motif repeats four times, creating a wreath. Reuse this wreath to make a holiday hoop with custom text in the center, or use a single motif to add some colorful flowers to another project. Stitch the florals as suggested, or add additional flourishes and details, repeating your favorite elements and stitches.

- Have a lot of kids? Copy and resize the penguins to reflect your family. Add the date at the bottom to create a sweet, handmade keepsake.

- The long and short stitch color transition is very compact! You may only get a single row of each color squeezed along the necks of the penguins. I used two strands of thread to fill the penguins, but you can drop to a single strand to create a more delicate and detailed thread painting.

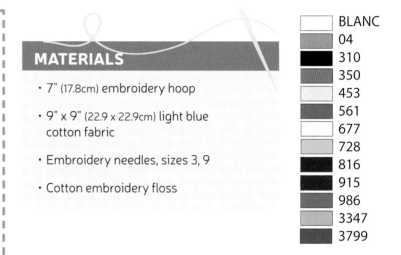

MATERIALS

- 7" (17.8cm) embroidery hoop

- 9" x 9" (22.9 x 22.9cm) light blue cotton fabric

- Embroidery needles, sizes 3, 9

- Cotton embroidery floss

	BLANC
	04
	310
	350
	453
	561
	677
	728
	816
	915
	986
	3347
	3799

Wreath

Use six strands of thread for all stitches

1. Create the roses using woven wheel stitch. Use DMC 350 for the larger roses and DMC 816 for the smaller ones. Create the stem with DMC 3347 using back stitch, leaving space for the daisies.

2. Fill the daisy petals. Use satin stitch with DMC 816 for the larger daisies and DMC 915 for the smaller ones.

3. Fill the front, larger leaves. Use DMC 986 with fishbone stitch. Similarly, fill the smaller leaves along the vines, and switch to single straight stitches to make the tiny leaves.

4. Fill the back, larger leaves. Use DMC 561 with fishbone stitch. Continuing with this green thread, create the branched leaves by first making the stem with back stitch. Use detached chain stitches to make the leaves.

5. Add small floral details. Use DMC 350 with French knots along the vine near the tiny straight stitch leaves. Use DMC 915 to make a cluster of French knots between the roses. Add fly stitch petals near the larger roses using DMC 915.

6. Complete the leaf details. With DMC 3347, use fern stitch next to the large rose. Add a straight stitch vein to the front, large leaf. Make straight stitch and detached chain stitch leaves surrounding the roses.

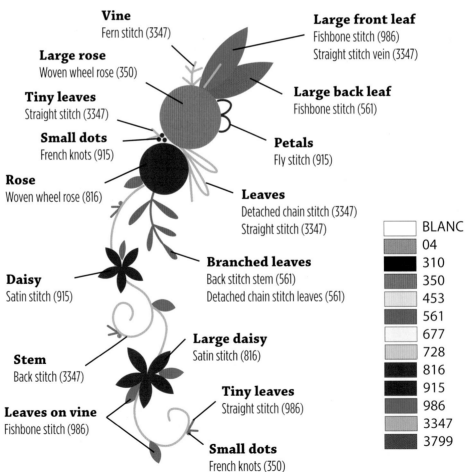

Vine
Fern stitch (3347)

Large front leaf
Fishbone stitch (986)
Straight stitch vein (3347)

Large rose
Woven wheel rose (350)

Large back leaf
Fishbone stitch (561)

Tiny leaves
Straight stitch (3347)

Petals
Fly stitch (915)

Small dots
French knots (915)

Rose
Woven wheel rose (816)

Leaves
Detached chain stitch (3347)
Straight stitch (3347)

Branched leaves
Back stitch stem (561)
Detached chain stitch leaves (561)

Daisy
Satin stitch (915)

Large daisy
Satin stitch (816)

Stem
Back stitch (3347)

Tiny leaves
Straight stitch (986)

Leaves on vine
Fishbone stitch (986)

Small dots
French knots (350)

BLANC
04
310
350
453
561
677
728
816
915
986
3347
3799

Penguins

Use two strands of thread unless otherwise noted

1. Make the line along the beak. Use DMC 728 with split stitch. Outline then fill the black sections on the head, back, and wing, using the diagram as a guide for stitch direction.

2. Outline the left side of the lower wing. Use DMC 04 with split stitch. Begin creating the color transition down the side of the neck with long and short stitch, starting with a small patch of stitches using DMC 728.

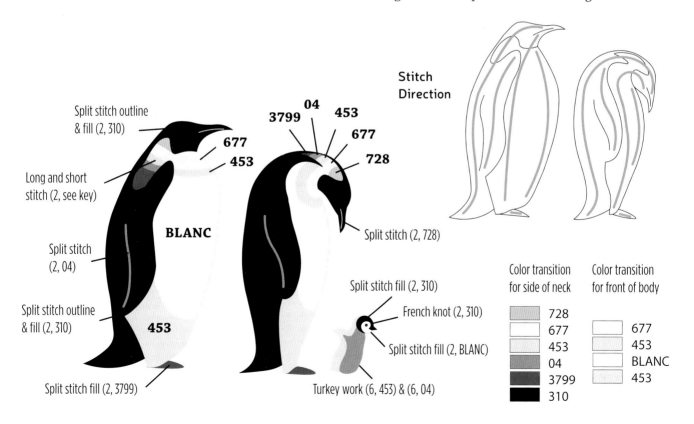

Split stitch outline & fill (2, 310)

677
453

Long and short stitch (2, see key)

BLANC

Split stitch (2, 04)

Split stitch outline & fill (2, 310)

453

Split stitch fill (2, 3799)

3799 04 453
677
728

Split stitch (2, 728)

Split stitch fill (2, 310)

French knot (2, 310)

Split stitch fill (2, BLANC)

Turkey work (6, 453) & (6, 04)

Stitch Direction

Color transition for side of neck
- 728
- 677
- 453
- 04
- 3799
- 310

Color transition for front of body
- 677
- 453
- BLANC
- 453

3. Use DMC 677 to blend down the space. Include the front body, being sure to thoroughly cover the fabric with long and short stitches.

4. Continue thread painting down the neck. Next use DMC 453, the lightest gray, before transitioning through the other grays (DMC 04 and DMC 3799) and finishing with black (DMC 310).

5. Fill the chest of the penguin in a similar manner. Use DMC 453 to transition from the light yellow (DMC 677) to white (BLANC). Fill the majority of the chest with BLANC using split stitch.

6. Fill the body. Use horizontal split stitch with DMC 3799. Finish filling the body with DMC 453, using long and short stitch to transition from white, and overlap the feet with a few split stitches.

7. Fill the head of the chick. Use split stitch with DMC 310 and BLANC, as shown in the diagram. Use DMC 310 to make a French knot eye.

8. Fill the penguin chick's body with Turkey work. Use six strands of DMC 04 for the right side. Use six strands of DMC 453 to fill the left side of the body with Turkey work. Add some tufts of the other color at the transition to try to blend between the two gray thread colors.

9. Trim the Turkey work. This will create a fluffy penguin chick.

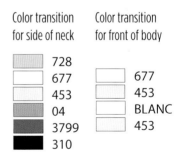

Color transition for side of neck
- 728
- 677
- 453
- 04
- 3799
- 310

Color transition for front of body
- 677
- 453
- BLANC
- 453

Festive Feathers

For our first stumpwork wire slip project, we are filling detached wings with floral stitches. These dimensional wings will be paired with folksy red birds, resulting in a very special piece of hoop art. Enjoy using a red variegated thread as suggested, or grab any other color(s) to change the season and feel of the finished work. To exaggerate the holiday vibe, try adding red beads, sequins, or some metallic threads.

Tips and ideas:

- If you cannot find the DMC Color Variations variegated thread I used, you can recreate it with a mix of these solid DMC colors: 815, 321, and 3801.

- To simplify the project, skip the wire slips and use the included pattern variation to stitch the wings directly on the main fabric.

MATERIALS

- 6" (15.2cm) embroidery hoop

- 4" (10.2cm) embroidery hoop

- 8" x 8" (20.3 x 20.3cm) taupe cotton fabric

- 6" x 6" (15.2 x 15.2cm) taupe cotton fabric

- Embroidery needles, sizes 3, 6, 9

- Cotton embroidery floss

- (2) 7" (17.8cm) cotton-covered wire, size 30 gauge

- Fabric glue

- Red archival ink pen

- Large needle, such as a darner

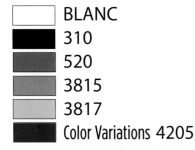

BLANC

310

520

3815

3817

Color Variations 4205

Birds

1. Hoop up the main fabric. Pair the 6" (15.2cm) embroidery hoop with the 8" x 8" (20.3 x 20.3cm) taupe cotton fabric.

2. Create the eyes and beaks. Use three strands of DMC 310 with satin stitch. Use six strands of BLANC to outline the eyes with back stitch.

3. Outline the birds. Use back stitch with six strands of DMC 4205. Fill the neck stripe on the left bird with rows of back stitch. Make the stripes on the tail of the right bird with back stitch.

4. Add the white details. Using six strands of BLANC, make the straight stitch head stripes and tiny running stitch belly spots on the left bird. Add white stripes to the tail using two rows of back stitch. Outline each stripe with back stitch using six strands of DMC 4205.

5. Outline the eye patch on the right bird. Use back stitch and then fill with satin stitch using six strands of DMC 4205. Use detached chain stitches to create the spots of the chest with six strands of BLANC.

6. Make the legs and feet. Use six strands of DMC 310 with back stitch for the long legs of the left bird. Use straight stitches for the feet and the short legs of the right bird. If desired, this step could be completed after making the florals, so the feet are stitched over the branches.

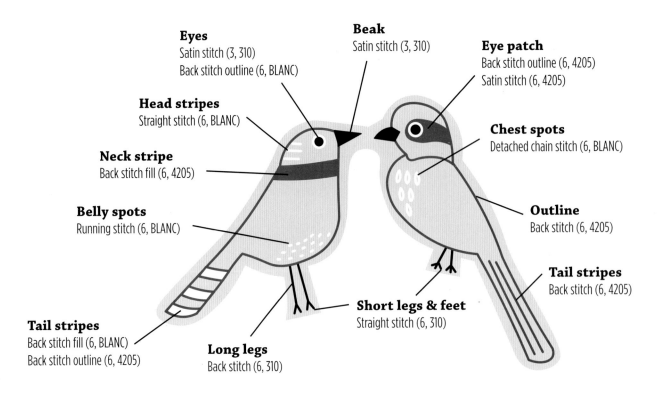

Eyes
Satin stitch (3, 310)
Back stitch outline (6, BLANC)

Beak
Satin stitch (3, 310)

Eye patch
Back stitch outline (6, 4205)
Satin stitch (6, 4205)

Head stripes
Straight stitch (6, BLANC)

Neck stripe
Back stitch fill (6, 4205)

Chest spots
Detached chain stitch (6, BLANC)

Belly spots
Running stitch (6, BLANC)

Outline
Back stitch (6, 4205)

Tail stripes
Back stitch fill (6, BLANC)
Back stitch outline (6, 4205)

Short legs & feet
Straight stitch (6, 310)

Long legs
Back stitch (6, 310)

Tail stripes
Back stitch (6, 4205)

Florals

1. Fill the leaves. Use long and short stitch with three strands of thread. Use DMC 3817 at the center and DMC 3815 at the edges, referring to the diagram for stitch direction. Extend the darker green stitches beyond the guideline of the leaf to create an uneven edge.

2. Create the chain stitch branches. Use six strands of DMC 520. Switch to split stitch for the leaf stems.

3. Make the red flowers. Use six strands of DMC 4205 to make French knots for the mini flowers and the flower centers. Use straight stitches for the petals. Add as many flowers as you like.

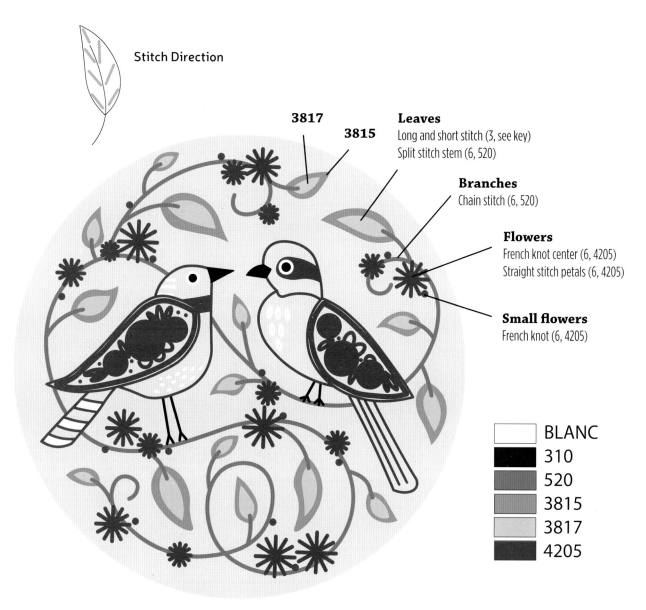

Stitch Direction

3817

3815

Leaves
Long and short stitch (3, see key)
Split stitch stem (6, 520)

Branches
Chain stitch (6, 520)

Flowers
French knot center (6, 4205)
Straight stitch petals (6, 4205)

Small flowers
French knot (6, 4205)

	BLANC
	310
	520
	3815
	3817
	4205

Wings

1. **Hoop up the detached element fabric.** Pair the 4" (10.2cm) embroidery hoop with the 6" x 6" (15.2 x 15.2cm) taupe cotton fabric.

2. **Couch the wire to the fabric.** Use a single strand of DMC 4205. Continue with this thread, completely covering the wire with buttonhole stitch. Add a split stitch outline on the inside edge of the buttonhole stitch.

3. **Add an outline along the inner edge of the wire.** Use chain stitch with six strands of DMC 4205. Fill the large flowers with woven wheel rose stitch.

4. **Fill the wings.** Continue with six strands of DMC 4205, making fly stitches, detached chain stitches, and French knots. See the diagram for suggested placement. Choose to completely cover the fabric or leave some showing between the stitches.

5. **Remove the fabric from the hoop.** Carefully cut out the wire slips. Use a red archival ink pen to color any wire showing through or any frayed fabric along the wing edges. Apply fabric glue if needed to repair accidental cuts, to tame frayed fabric, and to secure the back side of the stitches.

6. **Insert the wire slip wings into the main fabric.** Place where designated. Secure them on the wrong side of the fabric, and shape the wings as desired.

Once the wire slip wings are cut out from the detached element fabric, the wire tails can be trimmed to about 1" (2.5cm) in length before inserting and attaching to the main fabric.

Lift the straight stitch petals away from the fabric using an embroidery needle to add extra dimension to the flowers.

Wire
Couching stitch to shape (1, 4205)
Buttonhole stitch to cover (1, 4205)
Split stitch outline (1, 4205)

Outline
Chain stitch (6, 4205)

Flowers
Woven wheel rose stitch (6, 4205)

Small flowers
French knot (6, 4205)

Petals
Detached chain stitch (6, 4205)

Petals
Fly stitch (6, 4205)

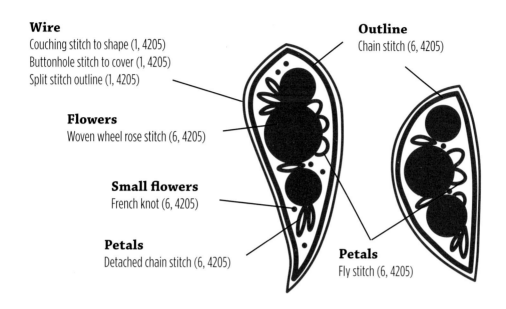

Want to show off your stumpwork skills? Use wire slips to create some of the leaves.

Monarchs in Love

Some designs come easily to me, and I'm able to stitch the original idea seamlessly without any errors or changes. This is not one of those projects! The design is very different from my original vision, but after multiple iterations, I am very happy with how it turned out. I really love the contrast between the butterflies and the intricate leaves behind them. I also love the heart shape created by the branches, something I didn't plan and didn't notice until after I finished the project!

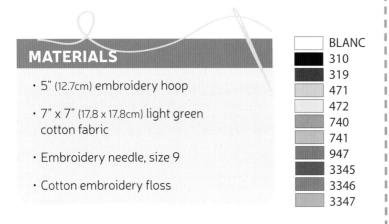

MATERIALS

- 5" (12.7cm) embroidery hoop

- 7" x 7" (17.8 x 17.8cm) light green cotton fabric

- Embroidery needle, size 9

- Cotton embroidery floss

☐	BLANC
■	310
■	319
☐	471
☐	472
■	740
■	741
■	947
■	3345
■	3346
■	3347

Tips and ideas:

- Use care in keeping your thread colors organized. The greens are very similar in hue and easy to mix up. Concentrate on creating a smooth transition from the darker greens at the bottom of the design to the lighter greens on top. The differences in hue are exaggerated in the color keys to help you to better see suggested color placement.

- There is a lot of overlap between the different elements in the design. You may find it easier to stitch the foreground element first, or perhaps you prefer to stitch the background leaves first.

- Some of the leaf fill stitches can be challenging. Substitute with back stitch fill, satin stitch, or split stitch fill if needed.

Butterflies
Use one strand of thread for all stitches

1. Fill the orange spots using satin stitch. Use DMC 741 for the areas at the top, and transition from DMC 740 to DMC 947 for the areas near the bottom of the wings.

2. Use DMC 310 to outline. Fill the wings and body with split stitch. A single straight stitch is all that is needed between many of the orange spots.

3. Create the antennae with back stitch, using DMC 310. Finish with BLANC, creating small straight stitches on top of the black split stitch to make the small white spots along the wing tips.

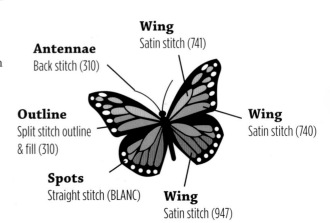

Wing
Satin stitch (741)

Antennae
Back stitch (310)

Outline
Split stitch outline & fill (310)

Wing
Satin stitch (740)

Spots
Straight stitch (BLANC)

Wing
Satin stitch (947)

Branches

Use two strands of thread unless otherwise noted

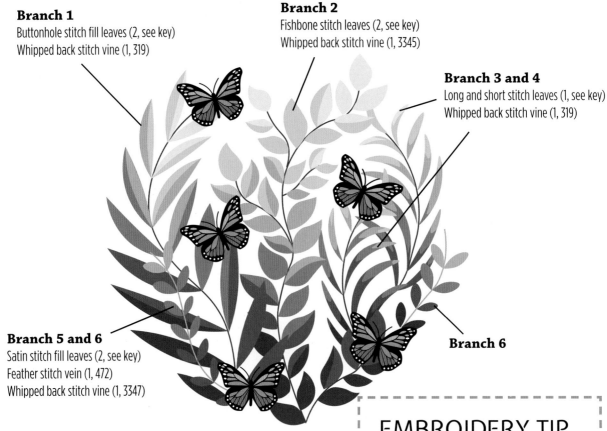

Branch 1
Buttonhole stitch fill leaves (2, see key)
Whipped back stitch vine (1, 319)

Branch 2
Fishbone stitch leaves (2, see key)
Whipped back stitch vine (1, 3345)

Branch 3 and 4
Long and short stitch leaves (1, see key)
Whipped back stitch vine (1, 319)

Branch 5 and 6
Satin stitch fill leaves (2, see key)
Feather stitch vein (1, 472)
Whipped back stitch vine (1, 3347)

Branch 6

1. **Fill the leaves on Branch 1 using buttonhole stitch.** Begin at the base of the leaf and treat each half as an independent shape. Use a single strand of DMC 319 with whipped back stitch to create the vine.

2. **Fill the leaves on Branch 2 with fishbone stitch.** Use two threaded needles to create the two-toned leaves. Use a single strand of DMC 3345 with whipped back stitch for the vine.

3. **Create the leaves on Branches 3 and 4.** Use long and short stitch with a single strand of thread. Use a single strand of DMC 319 with whipped back stitch to create the vine.

4. **Fill the leaves on Branches 5 and 6 with satin stitch.** Use a single strand of DMC 472 with feather stitch to add veins on top. Use a single strand of DMC 3347 with whipped back stitch to create the vine.

EMBROIDERY TIP

The leaves are filled using six shades of green, with the darker colors used at the bottom of the design and the lighter colors at the top. Refer to the diagram for suggested color placement.

Branch and leaf color transition

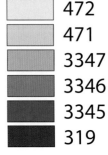

	472
	471
	3347
	3346
	3345
	319

Branch 1

Branch 2

Branch 4

Branch 3

Branch 5

Branch 6

Don't lose your butterflies! Once you've completed the branches, check that the butterfly wings are still sharply defined. Touch them up with split stitches using a single strand of black thread.

Desert Coyote

I grew up in the Pacific Northwest, surrounded by huge evergreen trees, the Puget Sound, and snowcapped mountains. I was nervous about our move to Arizona, but I've been dazzled by the beautiful and varied landscapes here. This project is inspired by the desert outside of Tucson, home to ancient saguaro cacti and a diverse animal population. And of course, I set the landscape to sunset, as that is when the most beautiful magic happens in the desert!

Stitch Direction

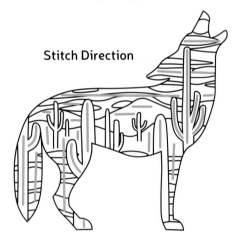

MATERIALS

- 5" (12.7cm) embroidery hoop

- 7" x 7" (17.8 x 17.8cm) light blue cotton fabric

- Embroidery needles, sizes 6, 9

- Cotton embroidery floss

	33
	161
	422
	501
	718
	989
	3712
	3820

The cacti are filled with rows of whipped back stitch. Keeping the whip direction consistent will result in a smoother texture. Alternate or randomize the direction to create more variety.

Coyote

1. **Fill the sky.** Use horizontal satin stitch with a single strand of thread. Begin at the top of the design and work down, using the color key for suggested color placement.

2. **Fill the mountains.** Use split stitch with a single strand of DMC 161. Keep this stitch direction horizontal.

3. **Fill the grass.** Use long and short stitch with two strands of thread, beginning at the top edge with DMC 501. Continue filling down with rows of split stitch, adding more DMC 422 as you work your way toward the bottom of the shape. Keep this stitch direction vertical. Follow the guidelines for color placement, or just randomly mix the colors as you fill the grass area. Choose to leave space for the cactus guidelines to show through or cover these lines and improvise the cactus placement in the next step.

4. **Create the cacti.** Use whipped back stitch with three strands of DMC 989. The smaller cactus arms can be created using only a single row while the thicker cacti may need six or more rows. Fill the larger cacti, starting on one edge and moving toward the other, so that you will not have to whip a center row of back stitch that is already surrounded by stitching on both sides.

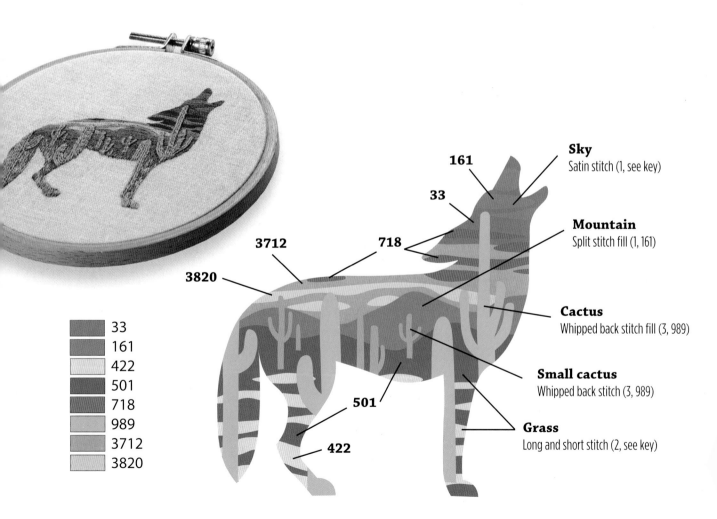

Color key:
33
161
422
501
718
989
3712
3820

Sky Satin stitch (1, see key)

Mountain Split stitch fill (1, 161)

Cactus Whipped back stitch fill (3, 989)

Small cactus Whipped back stitch (3, 989)

Grass Long and short stitch (2, see key)

Magic Snail

I love damp, mossy forests. Every inch is filled with a tiny, secret ecosystem, possibly inhabited by fairies and gnomes. I had a lot of fun exploring different embroidery stitches to capture the different textures of mossy ground cover. You may want to play with these stitches on a scrap hoop to get a feel for them before adding them to your project.

Tips and ideas:

- The foreground of the project is filled with a combination of textural stitches. Choose to replicate my exact stitch placement and color choices or improvise your own. I included two patterns for this design, one more complex and another very simplified. You may find it easier to use the simple version and improvise your own leaf and moss placement.

- I suggest forming the open picot stitches before the other mosses, as it can be difficult to weave your needle and avoid snagging other dimensional stitches.

- If you are finding it challenging to fill the snail shell with the spiral design, you can drop to fewer colors or switch to a back stitch fill. Another solution would be to enlarge the design.

Open base picot stitches are challenging to create amongst other dimension stitches. Create them first, then use the other stitches to fill in the spaces between.

MATERIALS

- 4" (10.2cm) embroidery hoop

- 6" x 6" (15.2 x 15.2cm) green cotton fabric

- Embroidery needles, sizes 3, 6, 9

- Cotton embroidery floss

	372
	469
	581
	640
	745
	890
	919
	935
	936
	3371
	3827
	3853

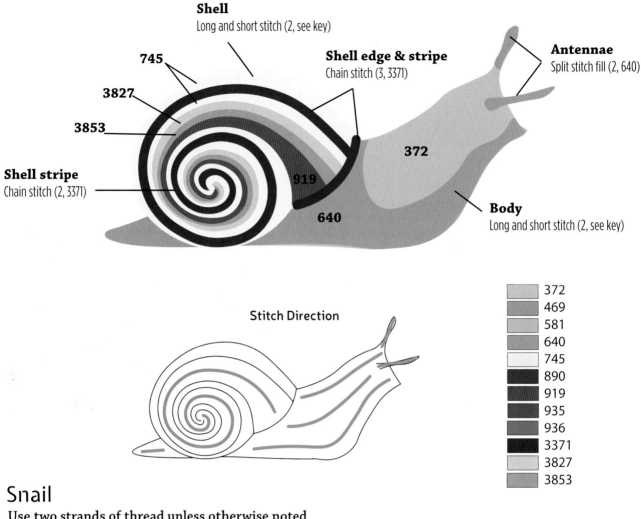

Shell
Long and short stitch (2, see key)

Shell edge & stripe
Chain stitch (3, 3371)

Antennae
Split stitch fill (2, 640)

745

3827

3853

Shell stripe
Chain stitch (2, 3371)

919

640

372

Body
Long and short stitch (2, see key)

Stitch Direction

	372
	469
	581
	640
	745
	890
	919
	935
	936
	3371
	3827
	3853

Snail

Use two strands of thread unless otherwise noted

1. **Make the snail body, filling with long and short stitch.** Use DMC 372 for the head and upper body, blending to DMC 640 for the shadows. Thicken the antennae with an extra layer of split stitches to help them stand out.

2. **Make the dark edge of the shell.** Use three strands of DMC 3371 with chain stitch. Similarly, make the dark spiral stripe. As you get closer to the center of the spiral, drop from three strands of DMC 3371 to two strands where the stripe gets skinnier.

3. **Fill the rest of the shell with long and short stitch.** Refer to the diagram for color placement and begin at the opening of the shell. Your stitch direction will gently curve along with the curve of the shell.

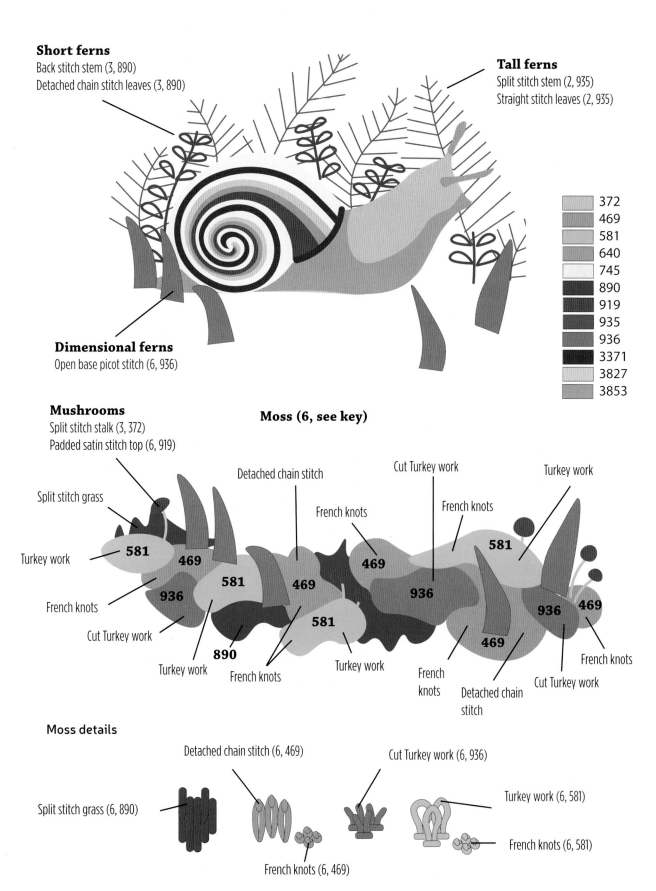

Short ferns
Back stitch stem (3, 890)
Detached chain stitch leaves (3, 890)

Tall ferns
Split stitch stem (2, 935)
Straight stitch leaves (2, 935)

Dimensional ferns
Open base picot stitch (6, 936)

	372
	469
	581
	640
	745
	890
	919
	935
	936
	3371
	3827
	3853

Mushrooms
Split stitch stalk (3, 372)
Padded satin stitch top (6, 919)

Moss (6, see key)

Split stitch grass

Turkey work

French knots

Cut Turkey work

Detached chain stitch

French knots

Cut Turkey work

French knots

Turkey work

581

469

936

581

469

890

581

469

936

581

469

936

469

Turkey work

French knots

Turkey work

French knots

Detached chain stitch

Cut Turkey work

French knots

Moss details

Split stitch grass (6, 890)

Detached chain stitch (6, 469)

Cut Turkey work (6, 936)

Turkey work (6, 581)

French knots (6, 469)

French knots (6, 581)

Have fun creating the mossy foreground of our snail embroidery project. Mimic the sample hoop or let your imagination guide color and stitch placement.

Plants

1. Make the dimensional ferns. Use open base picot stitch with six strands of DMC 936. Place as many of these stitches as you like throughout the project, varying their length.

2. Make the tall ferns in the background. Use two strands of DMC 935. Use split stitch for the center stems and straight stitches for the leaves.

3. Make the short ferns in the background. Use three strands of DMC 890. Use back stitch for the stems and detached chain stitch for the leaves.

4. Create tuffs of moss using Turkey work. Use six strands of DMC 581 to make short, uncut Turkey work loops. Use six strands of 936 to make patches of shortly trimmed Turkey work.

5. Make the remaining moss elements. Use six strands of thread for each color, which can be stitched in any order. Use DMC 890 to create split stitch grass, keeping the stitches vertical. Make patches of loose, messy French knots using DMC 581. Use DMC 469 to make clumps of vertical detached chain stitches and patches of loose French knots.

6. Finish with the mushrooms. Place as many as you like on top of the stitches created in the previous steps. Use three strands of DMC 372 to make the mushroom stalks out of split stitch, and use six strands of DMC 919 to make the tops using padded satin stitch.

Crowned Meerkat

I can't resist a cute animal wearing a floral crown! For this project, we get to adorn our meerkat with pretty flowers, including a thread painted flower created with wire slip petals. Use the stumpwork pattern again to make additional flowers for this critter or add them to another design.

Tips and ideas:

- Depending on your stitch tension and project size, you may need to vary the number of rows used to fill the shapes on the face. You can also swap between chain stitches and split stitches to better fill the space.

- I included an extra pattern for this project, which includes the large flower on the main fabric. Use this pattern if you want to skip the stumpwork petals. These petals can still be filled with long and short stitch, or you can match the texture of the meerkat and fill them with chain stitch or split stitch.

- Use the floral wreath from Penguin Family (page 117) to frame your meerkat, swapping in the colors from the floral crown.

- Copy and resize the pattern to make a family of meerkats. Leave room at the top for text to create a unique, custom gift or heirloom.

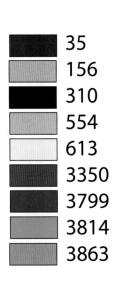

■	35
■	156
■	310
■	554
□	613
■	3350
■	3799
■	3814
■	3863

Stitch Direction

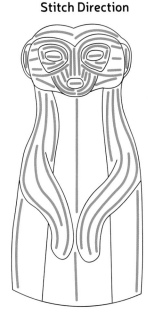

MATERIALS

- 8" (20.3cm) embroidery hoop

- 4" (10.2cm) embroidery hoop

- 10" x 10" (25.4 x 25.4cm) white cotton fabric

- 6" x 6" (15.2 x 15.2cm) pink cotton fabric

- Embroidery needles, sizes 3, 9

- Cotton embroidery floss

- (5) 5" (12.7cm) cotton-covered wire, size 30 gauge

- Fabric glue

- Pink archival ink pen

- Large needle, such as a darner

Meerkat

Use six strands of thread unless otherwise noted

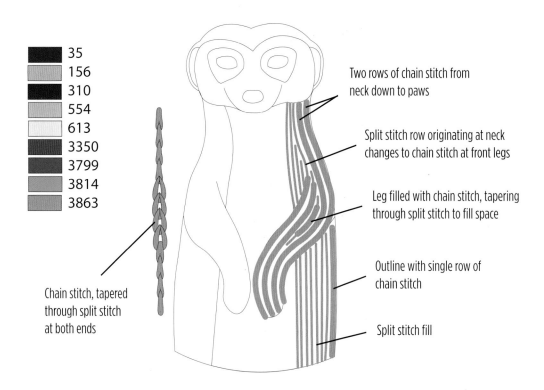

- 35
- 156
- 310
- 554
- 613
- 3350
- 3799
- 3814
- 3863

Two rows of chain stitch from neck down to paws

Split stitch row originating at neck changes to chain stitch at front legs

Leg filled with chain stitch, tapering through split stitch to fill space

Outline with single row of chain stitch

Split stitch fill

Chain stitch, tapered through split stitch at both ends

1. **Hoop up the main fabric.** Pair the 8" (20.3cm) embroidery hoop with the 10" x 10" (25.4 x 25.4cm) white cotton fabric.

2. **Fill the upper body with DMC 3863.** Begin with two rows of chain stitch, outlining from the neck down the upper side and front legs, then ending at the paws. The remaining rows that start at the neck are split stitch, but they switch to chain stitch at the front legs. Fill the rest of the front legs with chain stitch, tapering through split stitches at either end as needed to fill the gaps.

3. **Outline the lower side.** Add a single row of chain stitch using DMC 3863. Fill in the rest of the side fur with rows of split stitch.

4. **Create the light fur down the center.** Use DMC 613 to fill the rest of the body with split stitch.

5. **Fill the nose and eyes with satin stitch using DMC 310.** Use split stitch to fill the ears with DMC 3799.

6. **Outline the outer edge of the ears.** Use back stitch and DMC 3863. Outline the eyes with back stitch using DMC 3799. Fill the dark eye patches with chain stitch. Start at the inner eye corners, creating one row over the eye and a second row under the eye. See the color diagram and detailed stitch direction diagram for suggested placement.

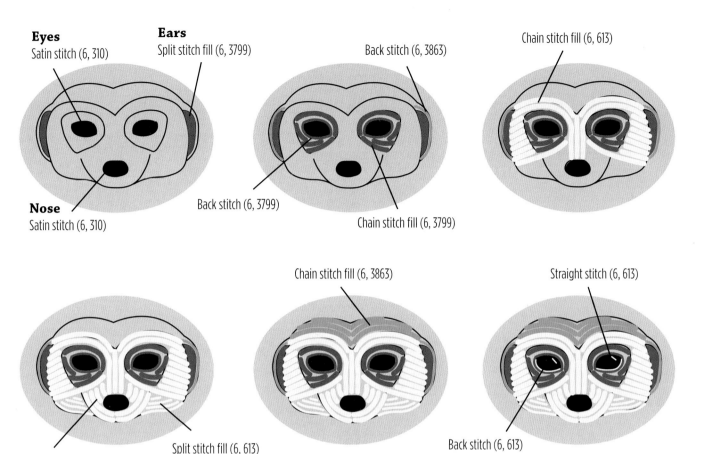

Eyes
Satin stitch (6, 310)

Ears
Split stitch fill (6, 3799)

Back stitch (6, 3863)

Chain stitch fill (6, 613)

Nose
Satin stitch (6, 310)

Back stitch (6, 3799)

Chain stitch fill (6, 3799)

Chain stitch fill (6, 3863)

Straight stitch (6, 613)

Chain stitch fill (6, 613)

Split stitch fill (6, 613)

Back stitch (6, 613)

7. Use DMC 613 to continue filling around the eyes with chain stitch. Begin with a center row from the nose to the forehead, again referring to the diagrams for suggested placement and direction.

8. Continue with DMC 613, filling the muzzle with chain stitch. Switch to split stitch to fill the remaining lower face. Fill the top of the head with chain stitch using DMC 3863.

9. Finish the eyes. Add straight stitch highlights and a back stitch outline using DMC 613. Use two strands of DMC 3799 to outline the body, head, and front legs with split stitch.

10. Create the roses with DMC 156 and DMC 554. Use any variation of woven wheel rose and open woven wheel rose stitch.

11. Use DMC 3814 to make the leaves with satin stitch. Add DMC 35 French knots throughout the flowers as desired.

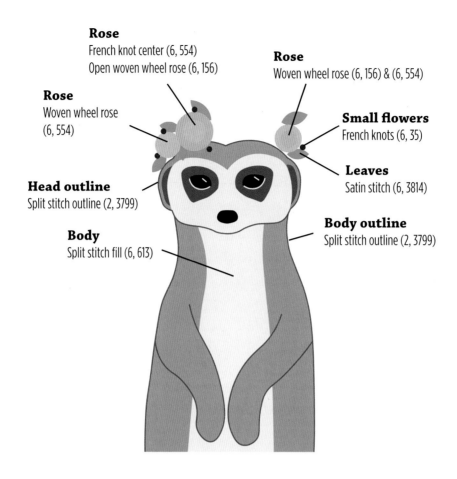

Rose
French knot center (6, 554)
Open woven wheel rose (6, 156)

Rose
Woven wheel rose (6, 156) & (6, 554)

Rose
Woven wheel rose
(6, 554)

Small flowers
French knots (6, 35)

Head outline
Split stitch outline (2, 3799)

Leaves
Satin stitch (6, 3814)

Body
Split stitch fill (6, 613)

Body outline
Split stitch outline (2, 3799)

Stitch Direction

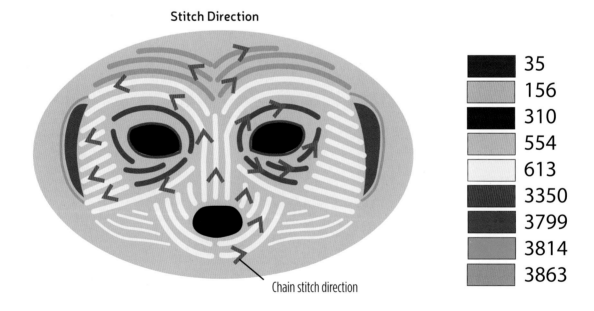

Chain stitch direction

	35
	156
	310
	554
	613
	3350
	3799
	3814
	3863

Stumpwork Flower

1. Hoop up the detached element fabric. Pair the 4" (10.2cm) embroidery hoop with the 6" x 6" (15.2 x 15.2cm) pink cotton fabric.

2. Couch the wire to the petal patterns. Use a single strand of DMC 3350. Cover the wire with buttonhole stitch and a single strand of DMC 3350, switching to a single strand of DMC 35 near the base of each petal. Outline this buttonhole stitch inside the wire using split stitch, matching the thread color.

3. Fill the petals with long and short stitch. Use two strands of thread, beginning with DMC 35 at the base and transitioning to DMC 3350.

4. Carefully cut the wire slip petals from the pink fabric. Give them a gentle curved shape. Secure the wires to the main fabric where indicated in the pattern. Each petal can be inserted in a unique hole near the center point of the flower.

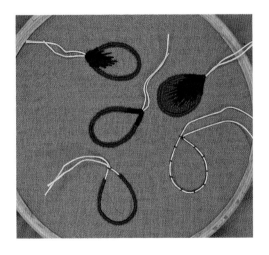

The five wire slip petals, each at a different stage in the creation process. Tape your wire ends to the fabric to avoid snagging them with your thread. Be sure to use the included pattern so all the petals are oriented with their wire ends directed away from the center of the hoop (unlike me!)

Wire
Couching stitch to shape (1, 3350)
Buttonhole stitch to cover (1, 3350) & (1, 35)
Split stitch outline (1, 3350) & (1, 35)

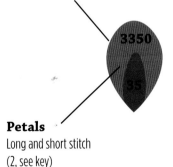

Gently curve your stumpwork petals, and arrange them so that each one is overlapping one of its neighbors. If any fabric is showing under the completed flower, add additional leaves to fill in the space.

Petals
Long and short stitch
(2, see key)

Chapter 9

Thread Painting a Menagerie

Put your skills into practice with these challenging thread painted projects. You will get to blend more colors and use fewer strands of thread to create realistic animal fur, and you'll find opportunities to add stumpwork elements to your design to create a three-dimensional work of art.

Axolotl Aquarium

When I first showed my husband this completed project featuring these endangered amphibians, he was in disbelief. Not because of my stitching skills, but because he did not believe that axolotls were real animals. They are close relatives of the tiger salamander, but they are special because they remain aquatic and keep their gills through adulthood. And that is lucky for us, because we get to stitch those fun pink gills with Turkey stitch!

MATERIALS

- 6" (15.2cm) embroidery hoop
- 5" (12.7cm) embroidery hoop
- 8" x 8" (20.3 x 20.3cm) blue cotton fabric
- 7" x 7" (17.8 x 17.8cm) green cotton fabric
- Embroidery needles, sizes 3, 9
- Cotton embroidery floss
- (4) 10" (25.4cm) cotton-covered wire, size 30 gauge
- Fabric glue
- Green archival ink pen
- Large needle, such as a darner

Tips and ideas:

- Use care to keep track of your thread colors while filling the axolotls with long and short stitch. The hues are very similar and easy to mix up.

- Add as many plants as you like to create a green haven for your axolotls. You can even duplicate the wire slip plants to add more greenery and dimensionality to the project.

- Save some time by skipping the wire slips, instead stitching the plants directly to the main fabric with the extra pattern included for this design.

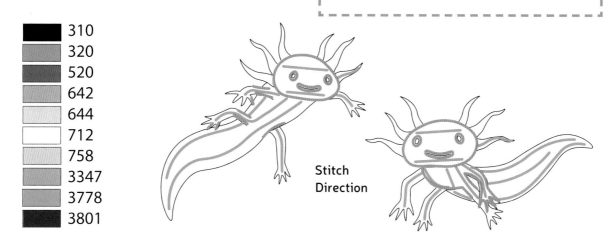

310	
320	
520	
642	
644	
712	
758	
3347	
3778	
3801	

Stitch Direction

Axolotls

Use one strand of thread unless otherwise noted

1. Hoop up the main fabric. Pair the 6" (15.2cm) embroidery hoop with the 8" x 8" (20.3 x 20.3cm) blue cotton fabric. Fill the eyes with satin stitch using DMC 310. Create the mouth using split stitch with DMC 3778.

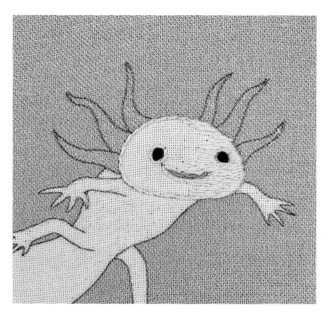

2. Outline then fill the head with split stitch using DMC 712. Keep the stitch direction horizontal, as shown in the diagram.

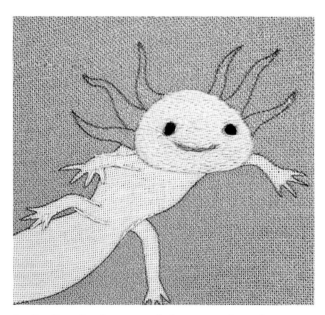

3. Outline the foreground elements where they overlap other parts of the body. Use any color with split stitch. Outline the legs and toes where they overlap the body, and outline the body where the legs come out from behind. Follow the stitch direction.

4. Fill the axolotl beginning with the shadows. Use DMC 642 with long and short stitch. I filled the body and legs at the same time, but you can also completely thread paint the body and each leg individually. Refer to the diagrams for suggested color placement and stitch direction.

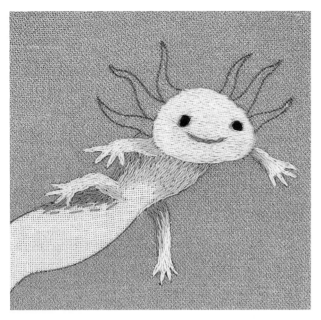

5. Continue filling the axolotl with long and short stitch. Blend from DMC 644 to DMC 712.

6. Fill down the tail. Bring back in some DMC 642 for the shadow along the tail.

7. Fill the gills with split stitch using two strands of thread. Start on the top edge with one to two rows of DMC 758 before switching to one to two rows of DMC 3778.

8. Fill the bottom row of each gill. Use a single line of cut Turkey work using two strands of DMC 3778 and one strand of DMC 3801 threaded on your needle.

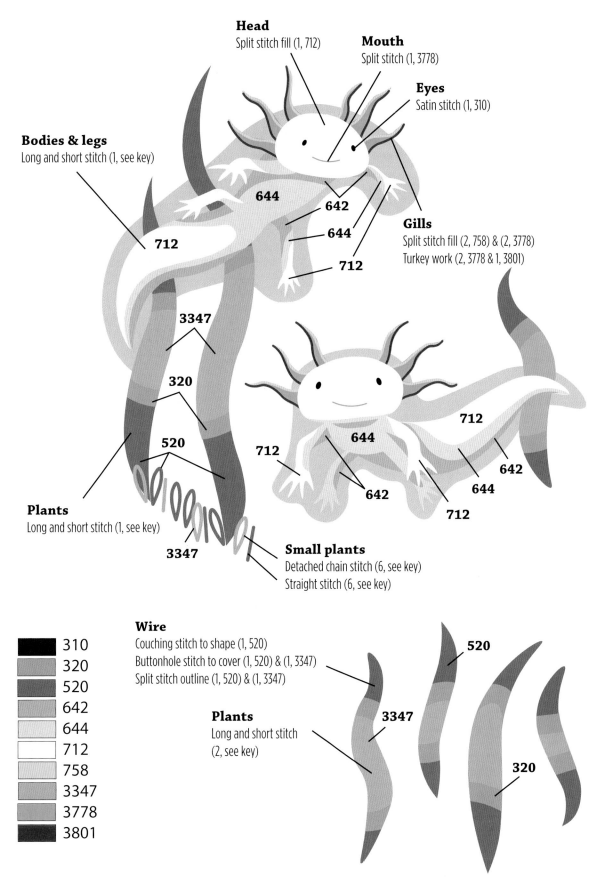

Head
Split stitch fill (1, 712)

Mouth
Split stitch (1, 3778)

Eyes
Satin stitch (1, 310)

Bodies & legs
Long and short stitch (1, see key)

644

712

642

644

712

Gills
Split stitch fill (2, 758) & (2, 3778)
Turkey work (2, 3778 & 1, 3801)

3347

320

520

644

712

712

642

712

644

712

642

Plants
Long and short stitch (1, see key)

3347

Small plants
Detached chain stitch (6, see key)
Straight stitch (6, see key)

▆	310
▆	320
▆	520
▆	642
▆	644
▆	712
▆	758
▆	3347
▆	3778
▆	3801

Wire
Couching stitch to shape (1, 520)
Buttonhole stitch to cover (1, 520) & (1, 3347)
Split stitch outline (1, 520) & (1, 3347)

Plants
Long and short stitch
(2, see key)

520

3347

320

Plants

1. Fill the background plants. Use long and short stitch with a single strand of thread. Start with DMC 520 at the bottom and transition to DMC 320 then DMC 3347. Blend back through DMC 320, and finish with DMC 520 at the top of the plants. Keep your stitch direction parallel with the edges of the plants.

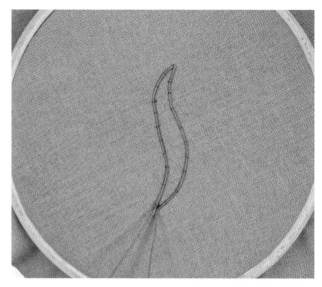

2. Hoop up the detached element fabric. Pair the 5" (12.7cm) embroidery hoop with the 7" x 7" (17.8 x 17.8cm) green cotton fabric. Couch the wire to the fabric using a single strand of DMC 520.

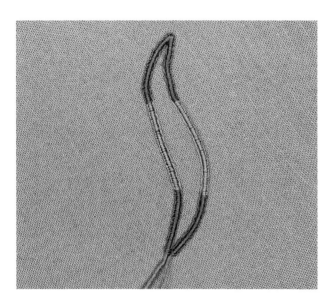

3. Secure the wire. Completely cover it with buttonhole stitch using a single strand of thread. Use DMC 520 at the tips of each leaf and DMC 3347 for the center section.

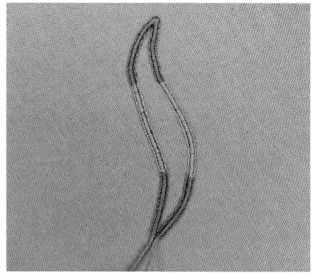

4. Tightly outline the buttonhole stitch. Use split stitch with a single strand of thread along the inside of each leaf. Match the thread color to the green used for the buttonhole stitches.

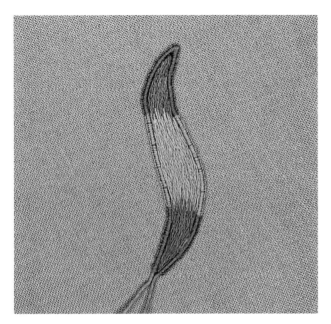

5. Fill each leaf. Use long and short stitch with two strands of green thread. Transition between the green thread colors as described in step 1.

6. Carefully cut out the wire slips. If needed, apply small amounts of fabric glue to the backs and edges of each leaf to help secure the stitches. Use a green archival ink pen to color any wire or fabric that shows through your stitching.

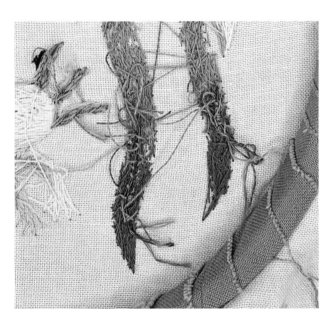

7. Insert and secure wire slips into the main fabric. Stitch the wires into the back sides of the stitches on the wrong side of the fabric.

8. If desired, add small plants. Use detached chain stitches and straight stitches along the bottom of the project using any green thread. These stitches can hide the bases of the wire slip plants. These plants are not indicated on the patterns, giving you the freedom to add as many as you like.

Blue Dragonfly

This project may be small, but it utilizes challenging techniques and special materials. To recreate the dragonfly's shimmer, we are using organza fabric for our wire slip wings and iridescent metallic thread for some extra sparkle. Take your time with this project. Combining wire slips with organza and metallic floss has the potential to test your patience! Get comfortable with good lighting and maybe even a pair of reading glasses, and enjoy the process.

Tips and ideas:

- While stitching on the organza fabric, use care when starting new lengths of thread and when anchoring threads. Be sure to weave these thread tails into the back of your stitches so they are not visible from the front.

- Use the back stitch stripes of metallic thread to cover any mistakes that show through the organza. Add as many of these stripes as desired, and don't worry about them matching from wing to wing.

- Begin the project in a 5" (12.7cm) hoop to extend the leaves beyond the edges of a 4" (10.2cm) hoop frame. Once hooped in the smaller frame, the leaves will disappear beyond the hoop and the wire slip wings will extend over the edge.

- If you can't find organza (or if you have an aversion to it), try a light blue fabric for your wings. Add extra stripes with your metallic thread to give them more sparkle.

- Yes, dragonflies do have legs. I decided to simplify the project by omitting them from this pattern. If you'd like to include them, use a single strand of black thread to make them out of split stitch.

MATERIALS

- 4" (10.2cm) embroidery hoop
- 5" (12.7cm) embroidery hoop
- 6" x 6" (15.2 x 15.2cm) green cotton fabric
- 7" x 7" (17.8 x 17.8cm) organza fabric
- Embroidery needles, sizes 3, 9
- Cotton embroidery floss
- Light blue metallic or iridescent embroidery thread, such as Lecien Opali #109, undivided (use full thickness)
- (4) 10" (25.4cm) cotton-covered wire, size 34 gauge
- Fabric glue
- Black archival ink pen
- Large needle, such as a darner

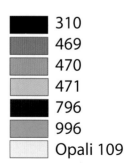

■	310
■	469
■	470
■	471
■	796
■	996
■	Opali 109

Dragonfly Body and Leaves

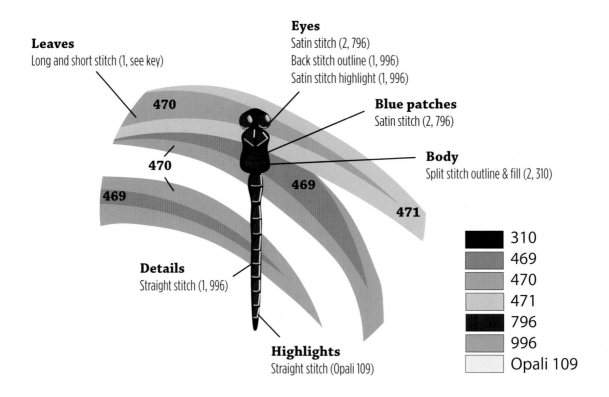

Leaves
Long and short stitch (1, see key)

470

470

469

Eyes
Satin stitch (2, 796)
Back stitch outline (1, 996)
Satin stitch highlight (1, 996)

Blue patches
Satin stitch (2, 796)

Body
Split stitch outline & fill (2, 310)

469

471

Details
Straight stitch (1, 996)

Highlights
Straight stitch (Opali 109)

- 310
- 469
- 470
- 471
- 796
- 996
- Opali 109

1. Hoop up the main fabric. Pair the 4" (10.2cm) embroidery hoop with the 6" x 6" (15.2 x 15.2cm) green cotton fabric.

2. Fill the eyes and the dark blue patches on the dragonfly. Use two strands of DMC 796 with satin stitch. Use any stitch direction you prefer.

3. Outline the dragonfly and the blue patches. Use two strands of DMC 310 with split stitch. Continue with the black thread, using it to fill the spaces with split stitch.

4. Add straight stitch details to the dragonfly. Use one strand of DMC 996 and follow the diagram. To make the eye highlights, use back stitch on the left sides of the eyes and satin stitch on top of the eyes.

5. Create the highlights on the right side of the body. Use straight stitches with light blue metallic thread. Add a straight stitch on top of the satin stitched eye highlights.

6. Fill the leaves. Use long and short stitch with a single strand of thread. See the diagram for suggested color placement using DMC 469, DMC 470, and DMC 471. Keep the stitch direction parallel with the leaf edges, and start stitching from either end of each leaf.

Wings

Wire
Couching stitch to shape (1, 310)
Buttonhole stitch to cover (1, 310)

Black lines
Split stitch (1, 310)

Sparkly lines
Back stitch (Opali 109)

1. Hoop up the detached element fabric. Pair the 5" (12.7cm) embroidery hoop with the 7" x 7" (17.8 x 17.8cm) organza fabric.

2. Couch the wire to the organza. Use a single strand of DMC 310. Continue with this black thread, completely covering the wire with buttonhole stitch. Use care to hide your thread tails by weaving them into the back of your stitches and trimming them short.

3. Create the black lines on the wings. Use split stitch with a single strand of DMC 310. Add as many lines as you like. Again, use care to hide your thread tails so they are not visible from the front of your work.

4. Add sparkly lines to the wings. Use back stitch with the metallic thread. These guidelines are not indicated on the pattern. Add as many as you like. The placement does not need to be identical between wings.

5. Carefully cut out the wire slips. If desired, add fabric glue to the back of your stitches to help secure them, avoiding the organza. Use a black archival ink pen to touch up any areas where the wire is showing through the buttonhole stitches.

6. Insert the slips into the dragonfly body. Follow where indicated in the diagram. Secure the wire tails on the wrong side of the fabric.

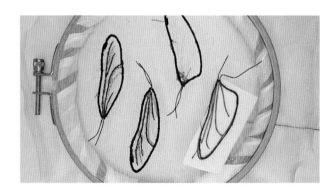

My first set of wings were messy! I didn't keep the back side of my work neat. I restitched the wings for the final project, but they are still not perfect. Remember this is a challenging design, and perfection is not the goal!

Raccoon and Wild Roses

To thread paint this raccoon, I start with a base layer of long and short stitch using two strands of thread. A detail layer is added on top using a single strand of thread. This layer acts to blend the colors of the base layer and add detail. These detail stitches are often simple straight stitches, but they usually split the stitches below them. Because of this splitting, and because we are using them to thread paint, I do refer to them as split stitches in the instructions for this project.

MATERIALS

- 5" (12.7cm) embroidery hoop
- 7" x 7" (17.8 x 17.8cm) gray cotton fabric
- Embroidery needles, sizes 3, 6, 9
- Cotton embroidery floss

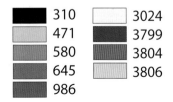

■	310	☐	3024
☐	471	■	3799
■	580	■	3804
■	645	☐	3806
■	986		

Tips and ideas:

- I think it is interesting to compare this project to Ringtail (page 110). The animals look similar, but we are using two very different techniques to recreate their fur. Both styles are lovely and valid. Try both and see which you prefer.

- For the pictured sample hoop, I stitched the leaves and flowers first then stitched the raccoon. You may choose to do the opposite, stitching the fur around the leaf guidelines and then stitching the leaves on top. Either way, the small leaves that cross over the body may sink into the stitched fur. To compensate, either stitch the leaves with more strands of thread (up to four or six strands) or stitch a second layer on top of the leaves as needed to help them pop out above the fur.

- Add extra plants and flowers in front of the raccoon if you need to hide mistakes or tricky spots.

- If preferred, stitch the entire raccoon using a single strand of thread, and combine the base and detail layers into a single layer of thread painting.

- Some of the plants are in front of our raccoon and others are behind. It is not always clear which element to stitch first. Experiment and see what works best for you.

Plants
Use two strands of thread unless otherwise noted

Large leaves
Satin stitch fill (3 strands, 986)
Back stitch stem (3 strands, 986)
Wheatear stitch details (1 strand, 580)
French knots (6 strands, 3806)

Flowers
Satin stitch fill (2 strands, 3804)
Straight stitch details (1 strand, 3806)
French knot centers (2 strands, 471)

Small leaves
Back stitch fill half (2 strands, 580)
Satin stitch fill half (2 strands, 471)
Back stitch stem (2 strands, 580)

■	310
▨	471
▨	580
▨	645
▨	986
▨	3024
▨	3799
▨	3804
▨	3806

Stitch Direction

1. Fill the large leaves. Use three strands of DMC 986 to fill with satin stitch. With the same color, create the stems using back stitch. Create details on top of each leaf using a single strand of DMC 580. Use wheatear stitch or substitute with straight stitches for simplicity. Use a full six strands of DMC 3806 to make clumps of French knots along the branch.

2. Fill one half of each small leaf. Use back stitch with DMC 580, keeping the stitch direction parallel with the center line of the leaf. Fill the other half with a diagonal satin stitch, using DMC 471. Use DMC 580 to create the stems with back stitch. The small leaves crossing over the body of the raccoon can be stitched after completing the fur.

3. Fill the flower petals. Use satin stitch with DMC 3804. Add straight stitch details on top, near the base of each petal, using a single strand of DMC 3806. Fill the flower centers with French knots using DMC 471.

Raccoon Base Layer
Use two strands of thread for all stitches

1. **Fill the body with split stitch using DMC 645.** Begin near the head and fill down toward the tail. Optionally, combine a strand of DMC 645 and a strand of DMC 310 on your needle to fill the darker fur concentrated along the center line of the body.

2. **Fill the eyes and nose.** Use padded satin stitch with DMC 310.

3. **Pad the ear tips with split stitch using DMC 3024.** Cover them with satin stitch. Fill the centers of the ears with split stitch using DMC 310.

4. **Begin filling the face with long and short stitch.** Start near the nose with DMC 3024, work through the eye mask using DMC 310, and move up to the top of the head with DMC 3024 then DMC 645. Use the diagrams as a guide for stitch direction and color placement.

5. **Fill the tail.** Begin at the tip and work toward the body, switching between DMC 310 and DMC 3024 to make stripes.

Head
Long and short stitch (see key)

3024

310

Body
Split stitch fill (645)

Tail
Long and short stitch (see key)

645

Ears
Split stitch outline (3024)
Satin stitch tips (3024)
Split stitch fill center (310)

Eyes & nose
Padded satin stitch (310)

310

3024

Stitch Direction

Raccoon Detail Layer

Use one strand of thread for all stitches

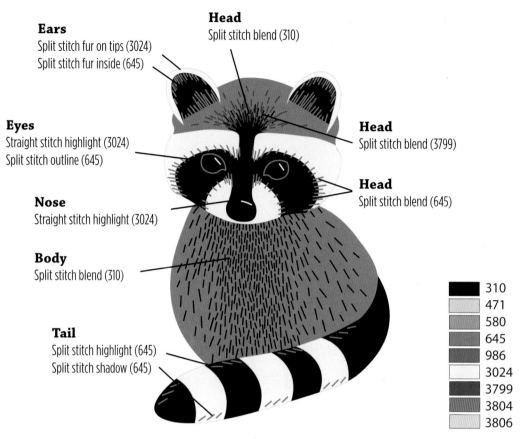

Ears
Split stitch fur on tips (3024)
Split stitch fur inside (645)

Head
Split stitch blend (310)

Eyes
Straight stitch highlight (3024)
Split stitch outline (645)

Head
Split stitch blend (3799)

Nose
Straight stitch highlight (3024)

Head
Split stitch blend (645)

Body
Split stitch blend (310)

Tail
Split stitch highlight (645)
Split stitch shadow (645)

■	310
▨	471
▨	580
▨	645
▨	986
□	3024
▨	3799
▨	3804
▨	3806

1. **Blend the black fur on the nose bridge.** Go up into the DMC 645 fur on the head using split stitches of DMC 310 and DMC 3799. Similarly, add black split stitches to the body to darken the fur.

2. **Create highlights on the eyes and nose.** Use DMC 3024 with straight stitch. Add additional straight stitches on the ear tips, creating wispy stray hairs.

3. **Outline the eyes with split stitch using DMC 645.** Outline the eyes with split stitch using DMC 645. Add additional gray stitches, overlapping the black fur inside the ears near the tips and at the base of the ears.

4. **Blend the black eye mask fur into the white fur.** Work above and below with DMC 645 split stitches.

5. **Create highlights on the black tail stripes.** Use split stitches of DMC 645. Similarly, create shadows on the white tail stripes.

Overlap stitches on the face to achieve a natural fur pattern.

Berry Patch Bunny

This adorable project may be small, but it is full of tiny details that pull you into this sweet scene. By using Turkey work, padded satin stitch, and loose straight stitches, we create highly dimensional florals and berries that complement the lifelike thread painted bunny. The finished embroidery makes for a thoughtful gift for new nurseries and Easter baskets.

Tips and ideas:

- This design is sized for a 4" (10.2cm) embroidery hoop, and it includes many tiny details. Drop down to fewer strands of thread if you find it challenging to fit in all your stitches. Alternatively, you can enlarge the design.

- The small strawberry plant flowers and the grass are not included on the pattern. Add as much as you like, using them to hide any mistakes and to add more color and depth to the design.

- The tiny strawberries and bees would look adorable stitched on clothes! Embroider them on your shirt collars to add sweet details to your wardrobe.

The bees are so tiny! The bodies are made with a single, small straight stitch of yellow thread. Have fun adding as many bees as you'd like to your project.

MATERIALS

- 4" (10.2cm) embroidery hoop

- 6" x 6" (15.2 x 15.2cm) off-white cotton fabric

- Embroidery needles, sizes 3, 6, 9

- Cotton embroidery floss

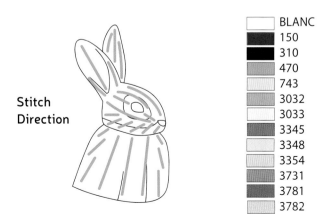

Stitch Direction

☐	BLANC
■	150
■	310
☐	470
☐	743
☐	3032
☐	3033
☐	3345
☐	3348
☐	3354
☐	3731
☐	3781
☐	3782

Bunny

Use two strands of thread unless otherwise noted

Base Layer

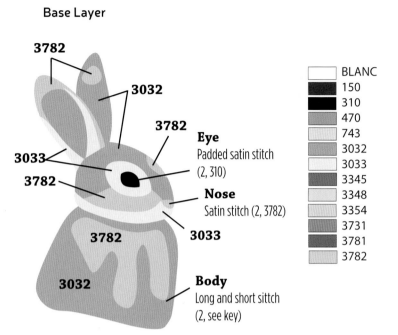

3782

3032

3782

3033

3782

Eye
Padded satin stitch (2, 310)

Nose
Satin stitch (2, 3782)

3782

3033

3032

Body
Long and short sittch (2, see key)

☐	BLANC
■	150
■	310
■	470
☐	743
■	3032
☐	3033
■	3345
☐	3348
☐	3354
■	3731
■	3781
☐	3782

Detail Layer

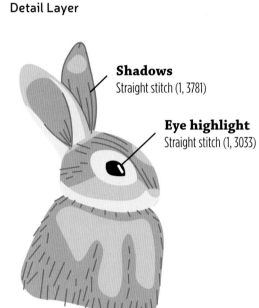

Shadows
Straight stitch (1, 3781)

Eye highlight
Straight stitch (1, 3033)

1. **Create the eye.** Use padded satin stitch with DMC 310. Use DMC 3782 to create the nose with satin stitch.

2. **Fill the bunny body with long and short stitch.** Refer to the diagram for suggested stitch direction. Begin with DMC 3032 at the neck and work down, switching to DMC 3782 for the light patches. Leave gaps in the fur for the flowers that overlap the body, so some of the pattern is visible for later steps. Alternatively, cover these guidelines and improvise the overlapping flowers and leaves.

3. **Fill the head.** Start near the nose and work toward the back of the head and the ears. Choose to leave gaps in the fur for the flower crown or stitch over these guidelines. Stitch DMC 3033 along the bottom of the head, extending over the neck, so they overlap the body.

4. **Create shadows and definition.** Use a single strand of DMC 3781 to add straight stitches or split stitches as suggested in the diagram. Add a straight stitch highlight in the eye with one strand of DMC 3033.

Keep your straight stitches very loose when making the strawberry plant flower petals. Place your needle under each stitch and gently pull up any slack to create more volume.

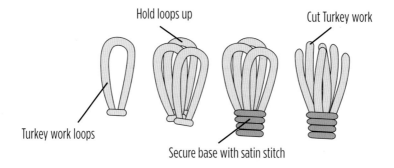
Berry Patch

1. Create the stems of the pink flowering plants. Use three strands of DMC 3345 with back stitch. Fill the leaves with satin stitch, again using three strands of DMC 3345.

2. Create the pink flower petals out of straight stitches. Use six strands, concentrating DMC 3354 near the bottom of the plant, and DMC 3731 and DMC 150 near the top. Each flowers is created using five straight stitch petals that intersect at the flower center. Add one of these flowers to the floral crown with DMC 3731.

3. Make the flower buds and fill in gaps. Use six strands of DMC 150 to make the straight stitch buds at the tops of the plants. Fill in any gaps with partial flowers made of straight stitches, using the lighter pink toward the bottom of the plant and red toward the top.

4. Create the strawberry plant leaves. Use two strands of DMC 3345 with fishbone stitch. Add straight stitch stripes with one strand of DMC 470. In a similar manner, fill the leaves of the floral crown.

5. Create the strawberries. Use six strands of DMC 150 with padded satin stitch. Use six strands of DMC 470 to create the straight stitch leaves on top of the berries. Come up through the berries and go down at the top of the berry, using very gentle tension to keep the volume of the berries from collapsing. Add the seeds, using one strand of DMC 3033 and making very small, very loose straight stitches on top of the berries.

6. Create the strawberry flower centers. Use a French knot with six strands of DMC 743. The white petals are created out of loose straight stitches with six strands of BLANC. The strawberry flowers are not noted on the design; I used my strawberry flowers to fill in any odd gaps. Use the sample hoop as a guide for placement or place yours as needed.

7. Create the dandelion flowers. Use six strand of DMC 743 to make Turkey work flowers (see the tip box above). Skip this step for the daffodil in the flower crown, letting the Turkey work stitches in that flower stick straight out from the fabric. Create the stems with whipped back stitch. Add small straight stitch leaves near the flower base using three strands of DMC 470.

8. Create the straight stitch grass. Use two strands of DMC 3348. Add additional grass using one strand of DMC 470. Use the grass to fill in the spaces below the bunny and between the plants. Decide how to make the grass: I left space between the blades for the fabric to show through, but you can fill more densely and to the edges of the hoop.

9. Make the bee body. Use a single, small straight stitch using six strands of DMC 743. Use one strand of DMC 310 to make the stripes on the body with loose straight stitches, using care to avoid flattening the yellow stitch. Continue with the single strand of black, making a tiny head using satin stitch, then creating antennae and legs using straight stitches. Finish with the wings, using one strand of DMC 3033 to make two straight stitches.

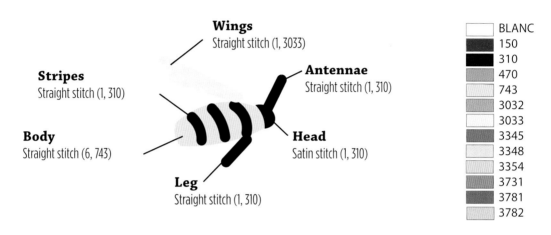

Wings
Straight stitch (1, 3033)

Antennae
Straight stitch (1, 310)

Stripes
Straight stitch (1, 310)

Body
Straight stitch (6, 743)

Head
Satin stitch (1, 310)

Leg
Straight stitch (1, 310)

BLANC
150
310
470
743
3032
3033
3345
3348
3354
3731
3781
3782

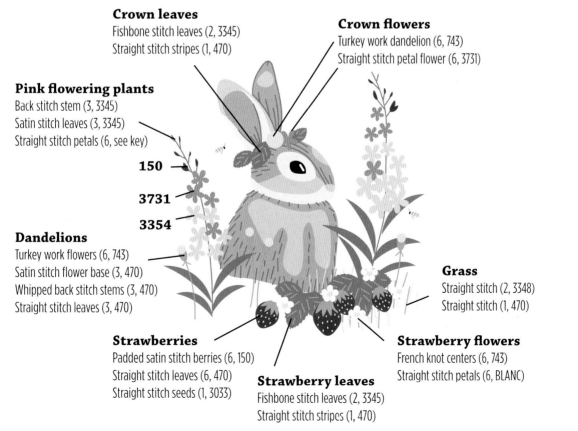

Crown leaves
Fishbone stitch leaves (2, 3345)
Straight stitch stripes (1, 470)

Crown flowers
Turkey work dandelion (6, 743)
Straight stitch petal flower (6, 3731)

Pink flowering plants
Back stitch stem (3, 3345)
Satin stitch leaves (3, 3345)
Straight stitch petals (6, see key)

150
3731
3354

Dandelions
Turkey work flowers (6, 743)
Satin stitch flower base (3, 470)
Whipped back stitch stems (3, 470)
Straight stitch leaves (3, 470)

Grass
Straight stitch (2, 3348)
Straight stitch (1, 470)

Strawberries
Padded satin stitch berries (6, 150)
Straight stitch leaves (6, 470)
Straight stitch seeds (1, 3033)

Strawberry leaves
Fishbone stitch leaves (2, 3345)
Straight stitch stripes (1, 470)

Strawberry flowers
French knot centers (6, 743)
Straight stitch petals (6, BLANC)

Tufted Titmouse Wreath

For this project, we are using thread painting combined with felt padding and trailing to create a realistic tufted titmouse. These little birds are easy to love with their big black eyes and cute mohawks. Use the illustrations for a general idea of color placement while stitching the bird, but be sure to blend well to avoid strict blocks of color. As with any kind of painting, it's okay to add more layers of color to recreate the detail of the feathers.

MATERIALS

- 6" (15.2cm) embroidery hoop
- 8" x 8" (20.3 x 20.3cm) light gray cotton fabric
- Embroidery needles, sizes 3, 6, 9
- 18" (45.7cm) lengths of cotton thread, as needed
- 4" x 4" (10.2 x 10.2cm) felt fabric
- Fabric scissors
- Cotton embroidery floss

Tips and ideas:

- To simplify the project, you can skip the padding and trailing. Alternatively, you can add extra layers of felt and thicker trailing to create even more dimension.

- The felt will cover the pattern guidelines once attached to your fabric. Do your best to recreate the tail and wing design, referencing the photos and illustration. It can help to sketch in some guidelines on top of the felt.

- There is plenty of room in the composition to add your own unique details, such as custom text or additional florals. To add some sparkle, swap in shiny red seed beads for the French knots.

- I used three lengths of size 3 pearl cotton for trailing. You can use any type of cotton thread in any color for the project. Add extra lengths to give the branches even more dimension.

	BLANC
	01
	03
	310
	355
	413
	414
	436
	437
	3021
	3787
	3857

Note the indentation created on the wing, separating the upper from the lower segment. Treat these two sections as different elements, with no stitches crossing over the guideline between them.

Wreath

1. Make the background branch. Use three strands of DMC 3021 to outline and fill with split stitch.

2. Add thickness to the foreground branch by trailing. I used three lengths of pearl cotton size 3, secured using two strands of DMC 3787. Create the thinner branches by trailing over six strands of DMC 3787. Create the skinniest branches by trailing over two strands of DMC 3787. Optionally, taper the trailing near the ends of the branches.

3. Add berries to the branches. Use six strands of thread with French knots. Use DMC 3857 for the berries on the background branch and DMC 355 for the berries on the foreground branch. Add as many as you like, using the diagram as a guide for placement, as the berries are not indicated in the pattern.

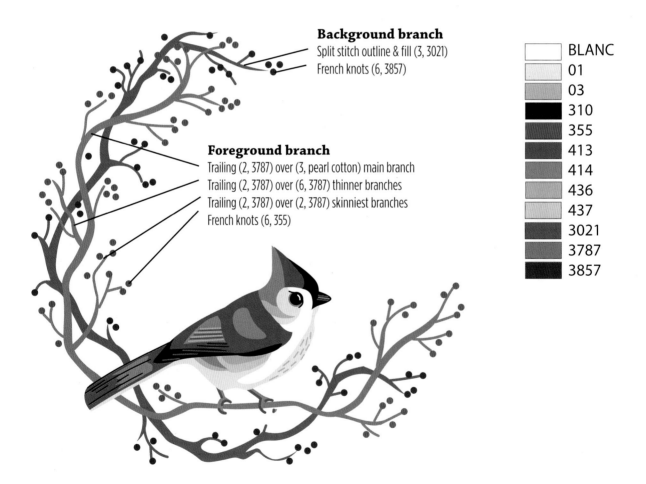

Background branch
Split stitch outline & fill (3, 3021)
French knots (6, 3857)

Foreground branch
Trailing (2, 3787) over (3, pearl cotton) main branch
Trailing (2, 3787) over (6, 3787) thinner branches
Trailing (2, 3787) over (2, 3787) skinniest branches
French knots (6, 355)

BLANC
01
03
310
355
413
414
436
437
3021
3787
3857

Consider doubling up on the tail padding where it overlaps the branches, using more felt or additional stitches. This padding will help the tail appear in front of the branches and will avoid the bumps seen in the sample hoop.

Tufted Titmouse
Use one strand of thread unless otherwise noted

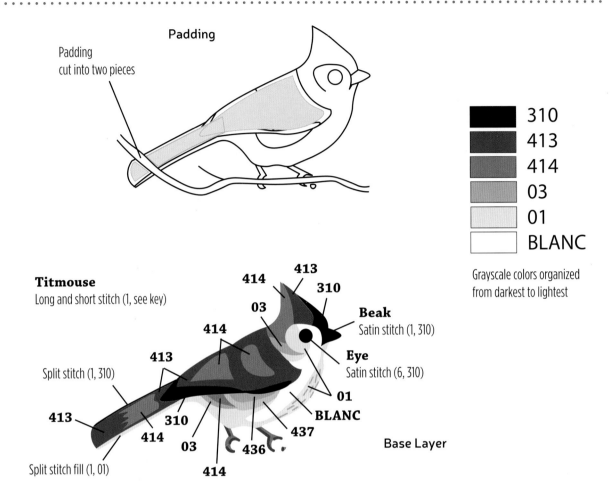

Padding

Padding
cut into two pieces

310
413
414
03
01
BLANC

Grayscale colors organized
from darkest to lightest

Titmouse
Long and short stitch (1, see key)

414 **413**
03 **310**

414

413

Split stitch (1, 310)

413 **310**
414 **03**

Split stitch fill (1, 01)

414

436 **437**

Beak
Satin stitch (1, 310)

Eye
Satin stitch (6, 310)

01
BLANC

Base Layer

1. **Cut out the felt for the tail using the pattern.** Use small straight stitches in any color to secure it to your fabric, starting near the body. Once the felt is adequately lined up on the guidelines, cut a section from the lower tail to accommodate the foreground branch, then continue to secure the felt.

2. **Cut out the felt for the wing using the pattern.** Secure the wing padding on top of the fabric, with some overlap over the tail padding. Because it now covers the pattern, you may want to sketch guidelines onto the felt to help with color placement when stitching the wings and tail.

3. **Outline the top edge of the tail.** Use DMC 310 with split stitch. Fill the bottom edge of the tail with split stitch using DMC 01.

4. **Fill the tail.** Begin near the body with long and short stitch using DMC 413. Blend with a DMC 414 highlight and then back to 413. As you work toward the end of the tail, you may need to add extra stitches to blend over the foreground branch. Add some split stitch stripes on top using DMC 310, focusing them more near the tail end.

Detail Layer

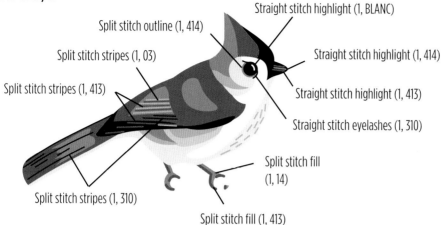

Split stitch outline (1, 414)

Straight stitch highlight (1, BLANC)

Split stitch stripes (1, 03)

Straight stitch highlight (1, 414)

Split stitch stripes (1, 413)

Straight stitch highlight (1, 413)

Straight stitch eyelashes (1, 310)

Split stitch fill (1, 14)

Split stitch stripes (1, 310)

Split stitch fill (1, 413)

Stitch Direction

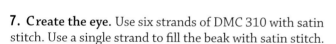

5. Fill the bottom edge of the wing. Use DMC 310 with split stitch. Use long and short stitch to fill the upper wing section with DMC 413, blending through a soft highlight of DMC 414.

6. Fill the lower section of the wing. Use long and short stitch with DMC 414, 413, and 310, referring to the diagram for color placement. Add split stitch wing stripes on top, as shown in the diagram, using DMC 03, 413, and 310.

7. Create the eye. Use six strands of DMC 310 with satin stitch. Use a single strand to fill the beak with satin stitch.

8. Outline and fill the feet. Use split stitch with DMC 413 and 414. Some of these stitches will go over and even through the trailed foreground branch.

9. Fill the head and back of the neck. Use long and short stitch, starting with DMC 310 near the beak and transitioning through the grays as you work up and around the eye. The stitches at the top of the head and at the back of the neck can be long and feathery. Be sure to create some overlap over the upper wing.

10. Fill the lighter area near the eye. Use long and short stitch with DMC BLANC and 01. Begin filling down the body, adding gray shadows and the warm tan spot, as shown in the diagram, and eventually meeting up with the DMC 01 of the tail. The stitches at the edges of the body can be a bit longer if desired, especially at the bottom where they will overlap the tops of the legs.

11. Outline the left and bottom sides of the eye. Use DMC 414 with split stitch. Add a straight stitch highlights to the beak using DMC 413 and DMC 414. Use DMC BLANC for the eye highlight. Finish with straight stitches of DMC 310, adding the eyelashes.

Posing Piglet

Our brains release happy hormones when we see something cute; therefore, I do not believe I need to justify my need to stitch adorable baby animals. Thread painting this piglet originally proved to be a bit of a challenge, as I found it difficult to find the appropriate thread colors. I'm glad I persevered because this little baby pig makes me so happy, and I especially love how the Turkey work grass adds dimension to the final piece.

Tips and ideas:

- I filled the piglet with long and short stitch using two strands of thread, returning with a single strand of thread to blend color and add details. The project can also be thread painted using a single strand from the start.

- I recommend closely examining your finished work, looking for any gaps in the fabric or unblended areas, and using a single strand of the appropriately colored thread to make corrections.

- The design includes overlapping elements. Use the directions below as a guide for suggested stitch order, but be flexible, returning to areas as needed. You may prefer to wait to stitch the flowers until the piglet is completed.

- The grass is not included on the pattern. Add as much as you like to your piece, leaving some fabric showing through or completely filling the space around the piglet.

Add as many tufts of Turkey work as you like. Cut them long or short, and don't be afraid to let them cover the piglet and the flowers.

MATERIALS

- 6" (15.2cm) embroidery hoop

- 8" x 8" (20.3 x 20.3cm) green cotton fabric

- Embroidery needles, sizes 3, 6, 9

- Cotton embroidery floss

BLANC	907
223	987
224	988
760	3371
761	3859
793	3860
819	3820

Flowers, Part 1

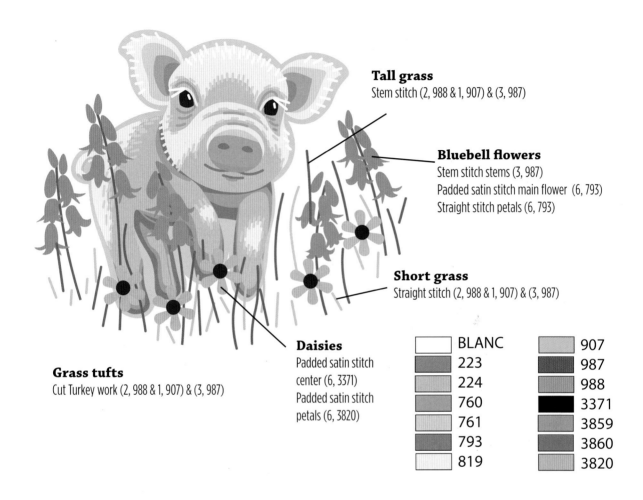

Tall grass
Stem stitch (2, 988 & 1, 907) & (3, 987)

Bluebell flowers
Stem stitch stems (3, 987)
Padded satin stitch main flower (6, 793)
Straight stitch petals (6, 793)

Short grass
Straight stitch (2, 988 & 1, 907) & (3, 987)

Daisies
Padded satin stitch center (6, 3371)
Padded satin stitch petals (6, 3820)

Grass tufts
Cut Turkey work (2, 988 & 1, 907) & (3, 987)

BLANC		907
223		987
224		988
760		3371
761		3859
793		3860
819		3820

1. **Make the bluebell flowers.** Use six strands of DMC 793. Use padded satin stitch for the main bodies of the flowers and straight stitches to create the smaller petals. Wait to stitch the smaller petals on the flowers that overlap the body until you've completed stitching the piglet.

2. **Create the daisies using padded satin stitch.** Use six strands of DMC 3371 to fill the centers using a horizontal stitch direction. Use six strands of DMC 3820 to create the petals, using a stitch direction radial from the flower center.

Piglet

Use two strands of thread unless otherwise noted

· ·

1. Fill the eyes. Use padded satin stitch with DMC 3371. Add a straight stitch highlight to each eye using a single strand of BLANC.

2. Use satin stitch to fill the nostrils with DMC 3860. Outline the nostrils and nose with split stitch using DMC 760. Use padded satin stitch to fill the nose, covering the split stitch and avoiding the nostrils. Use DMC 223 at the bottom of the nose as a shadow and DMC 761 at the top.

3. Create the smile with split stitch using DMC 3860.

4. Fill the ears with long and short stitch. Start near the face with DMC 223 and work out toward the edges through DMC 760, 761, and 819.

5. Fill the top half of the head with long and short stitch. Start between the eyes with DMC 224 and transition to DMC 819. Fill the area around the eyes with DMC 224.

6. Fill the rest of the head. Continue with long and short stitch, using DMC 224 and DMC 819 to work the area above the snout first then down under the chin.

7. Fill the body with long and short stitch. Start with the front legs and work from near the neck down toward the feet. Refer to the diagrams for suggested stitch direction and color placement. End with the back leg and tail.

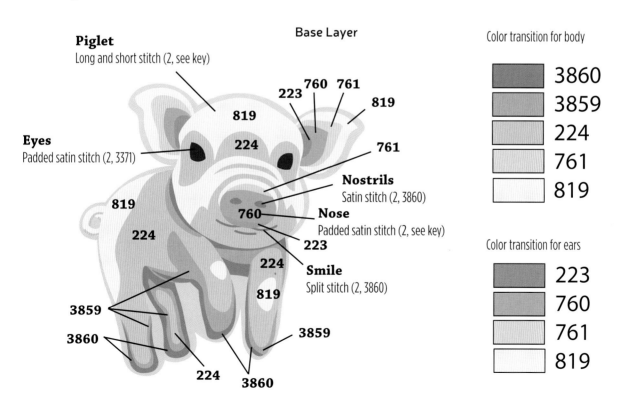

Piglet
Long and short stitch (2, see key)

Base Layer

Eyes
Padded satin stitch (2, 3371)

819

223 760 761

819

224

761

Nostrils
Satin stitch (2, 3860)

760

Nose
Padded satin stitch (2, see key)

223

Smile
Split stitch (2, 3860)

819

224

819

224

3859

3860

224

3860

3859

Color transition for body

	3860
	3859
	224
	761
	819

Color transition for ears

	223
	760
	761
	819

Detail Layer

Head
Split stitch blend (1, 761)

Wispy hair
Split stitch (1, BLANC)

Eyes
Straight stitch highlight (1, BLANC)
Split stitch outline (1, 819)
Split stitch lashes (1, BLANC)

Wispy hair
Split stitch (1, 819)

Head
Split stitch detail (1, 3859)

Body
Split stitch blend (1, 761)

Legs
Split stitch blend (1, 761)

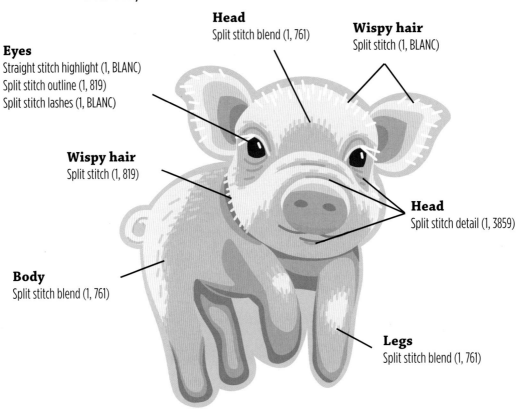

Stitch
Direction

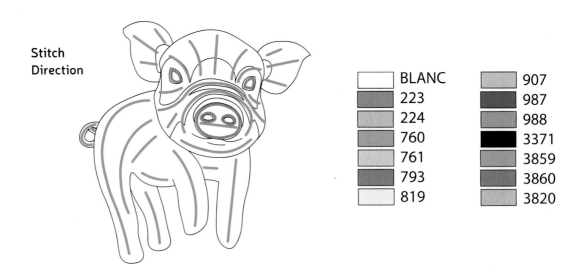

BLANC	907
223	987
224	988
760	3371
761	3859
793	3860
819	3820

8. Blend on the head and body. Use a single strand of DMC 761 and straight stitches to blend between DMC 224 and DMC 819. These stitches are splitting the long and short stitch, so they can be considered split stitches.

9. Add split stitch details. Add around the eyes, snout, and mouth using a single strand of DMC 3859.

10. Add wispy split stitch strands of hair. Add to the edges of the ears, top of the head, and right side of the face using one strand of DMC BLANC. Use DMC 819 for the hairs on the left side of the face that overlap the body.

11. Outline the top of the eyes. Use split stitch with a single strand of DMC 819. Add the eyelashes using split stitches with a single strand of BLANC.

Flowers, Part 2

1. Fill in the ground, using the diagram (page 178) as a guide. Fill in the short grass, long grass, and grass tufts using a combination of two strands of DMC 988 and one strand of DMC 907 threaded on your needle for the light-colored grass; use three strands of DMC 987 for the darker grass and the bluebell flower stems. Add more or less grass as desired.

2. Create the short grass using straight stitches. Use stem stitch for the tall grass and the bluebell stems. Use cut Turkey work to add small tuffs of grass as desired throughout the design.

Customize the flowers by swapping in other colors or other floral stitches. Use the flowers from the previous projects to inspire you.

Patterns

All patterns are at actual size as presented in the projects in this book. Feel free to resize; see the resizing guidelines on page 54.

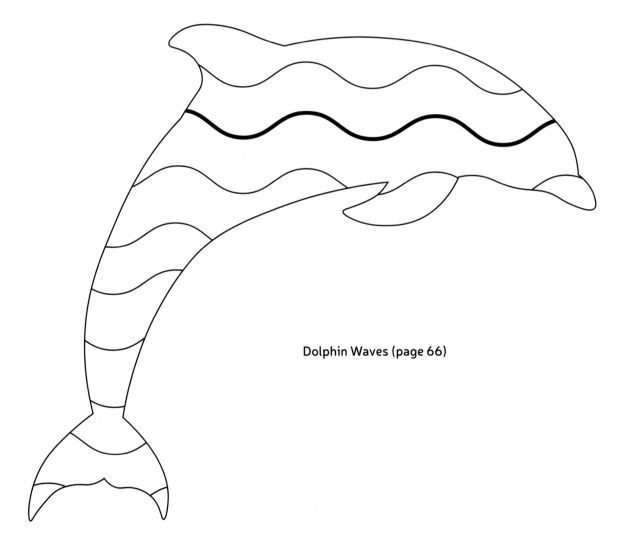

Dolphin Waves (page 66)

Seahorse Sampler (page 62)

Striped Gecko (page 84)

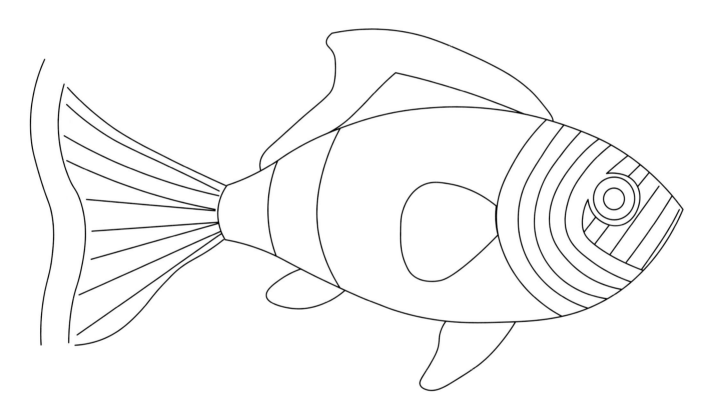

Fish Mosaic (page 73)

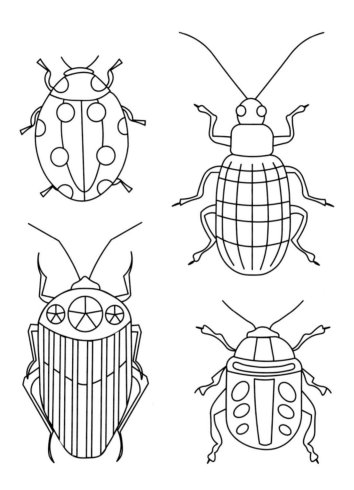

Beetle Collection (page 78)

Peaceful Doves (page 70)

Bluebird Sampler
(page 56)

Bumblebee Bouquet (page 98)

Rainbow Snake (page 90)

Wild Fern Deer (page 94)

Forest Elk (page 103)

Ringtail (page 110)

Festive Feathers (page 124), with stumpwork

Festive Feathers (page 124), without stumpwork

Penguin Family (page 117)

Monarchs in Love (page 130)

Mountain Bear (page 107)

Desert Coyote (page 134)

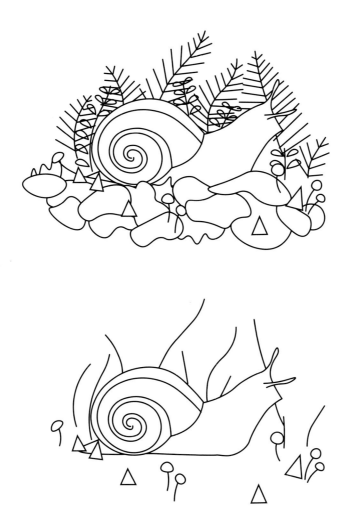

Magic Snail (page 137)

Crowned Meerkat (page 142), with stumpwork

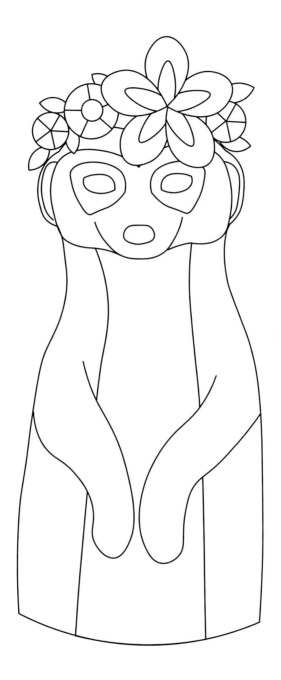

Crowned Meerkat (page 142), without stumpwork

Axolotl Aquarium (page 149), with stumpwork

Axolotl Aquarium (page 149), without stumpwork

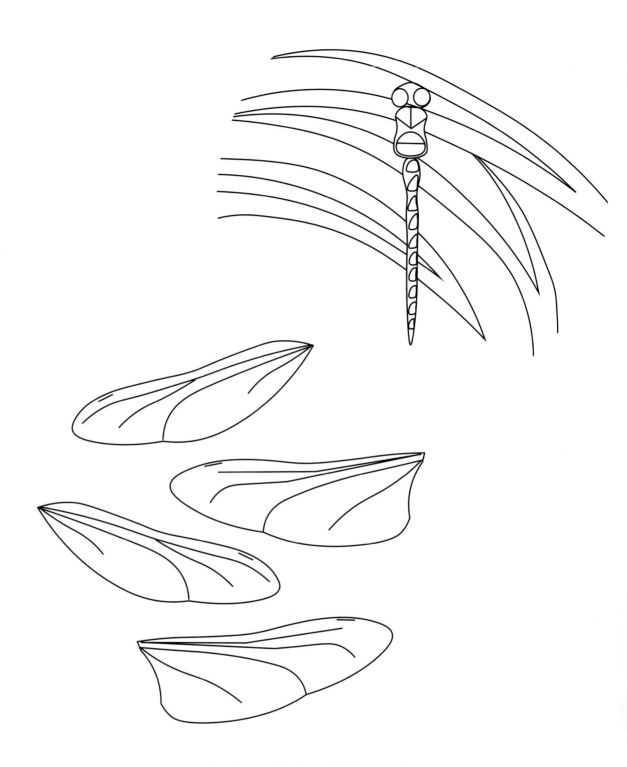

Blue Dragonfly (page 156)

Raccoon and Wild Roses (page 160)

Berry Patch Bunny (page 165)

Posing Piglet (page 176)

Tufted Titmouse Wreath (page 170)

Index

A

air-erase pen, 15
Anchor, 11
anchoring floss, 23
animals, beginner, 55–82
aquarium, 149
archival ink pen, 15
attached fly stitch, 31
axolotl, 149

B

back stitch, 31
    fill, 31
    whipped, 44
back-stitched chain stitch, 31
beads, 14
    adding, 24
    seed, 15
bear, 107
beechwood embroidery hoops, 11
beetles, 78
beginner animals, 55–82
beginner creatures, 83–115
    thread painting, 116–147
berries, 165, 170
birds, 124, 170
blanket stitch, 32
    double, 35
bluebird, 56
bouquet, 98
branches, 170
bumblebee, 98, 165
bunny, 165
butterflies, 130
buttonhole stitch, 32

C

chain stitch, 32
    back-stitched, 31
    checkered, 33
    detached, 34
    fill, 33
    raised, 39
    reversed, 40
    rose, 33

chalk pencil, 15
checkered chain stitch, 33
    tip, 33
clothes, embroidery on, 49
colonial knot, 34
color and stitch key, 52
    thread variations, 53
COSMO, 11
couching, 34
coyote, 134
creatures, beginner, 83–115
    thread painting, 116–147

D

deer, 94
desert, 134
detached chain stitch, 34
    fill, 35
DMC, 11
dolphin, 66
double blanket stitch, 35
doves, 70
dragonfly, 156

E

elk, 103
embroidery fabric, 10
embroidery floss, 11
    tip for using 6 strands, 13
embroidery hoops and stands, 11
embroidery needles, 12
embroidery stitches, 31

F

fabric, embroidery, 10
fabric glue, 14, 15
fabric marker, water-soluble, 15, 16
feather stitch, 35
felt, 15
    layering, padding, 25
fern stitch, 36
ferns, 94
fine-tip pen, 15
finishing in a hoop, 47
fish, 73

fishbone stitch, 36
floss, embroidery, 11
    anchoring, 23
    tip for using 6 strands, 13
    variegated, 12
flowers, 98, 117, 142, 160, 165, 176
fly stitch, 36
    attached, 31
    fill, 37
forest, 103, 137
frame, hoop, 17
French knot, 37

G

gecko, 84
gel pen, white, 15, 16
glue, fabric, 14, 15

H

hand embroidery needles, 12
hand embroidery stitches, 31
heat-sensitive pen, 15, 16
hoops
    and stands, 11
    beechwood, 11
    brass fittings, 11
    how to bind, 19
    spare, 16
hoop frame, 17, 47
hoop up, 17

I

iron-on patch, making, 49

K

knot
    colonial, 34
    French, 37

L

leaves, 130, 160
Lecien COSMO, 11
light board, 16
light tracing transfer, 21
linen blends, 10

lint rollers, 16
long and short stitch, 37
   tips, 37, 46
   using, for thread painting, 45

M

magnetic needle minder, 13
marker, water-soluble, 15, 16
materials and supplies, 10–16
meerkat, 142
mountain, 107

N

needle minder, magnetic, 13
needle-nose pliers, 14, 15
needles
   beading, 13
   chenille, 13
   darning, 13
   embroidery, 12
   large-eyed, 14
   milliner's, 13
   thread the, 18
needle threader, 13

O

open base picot stitch, 38
open woven wheel rose, 38
organza, 10

P

padded satin stitch, 38
padding, 14, 25
   attaching wool, 26
   layering felt, 25
padding key, 54
paintbrush, 15
pattern transfer
   heat and carbon methods, 22
   light tracing, 21
   other techniques, 22
   stabilizers, 22
   tools for, 15
patterns, 182–204
   how to read, 52
   using and resizing, 54
pen, 15
   air-erase, 15
   fine-tip, 15

heat-sensitive, 15
permanent, 16
white gel, 15
pencil, 15, 16
   chalk, 15, 16
penguin, 117
picot stitch, open base, 38
pig, 176
pincushion, 12, 13

Q

quilting cottons, 10

R

raccoon, 160
raised chain stitch, 39
raised stem stitch, 39
reading glasses, 16
reverse chain stitch, 40
ringtail, 110
rose chain stitch, 33
roses, 160
roving, 14
   attaching, 26
running stitch, 40

S

satin stitch, 40
   padded, 38
scissors
   embroidery, 16
   fabric, 16
   small, 14, 15
seahorse, 62
shadow box, 49
snail, 137
snake, 90
sorbello stitch, 40
split stitch, 41
   fill, 41
stab stitch. **See** straight stitch
stands, hoops and, 11
stem stitch, 41
   raised, 39
stitch and color key, 52
   thread variations, 53
stitch direction key, 54
stitch guide, 30–44

straight pin, 13
straight stitch, 42
strawberries, 165
stumpwork, (definition) 6
   supplies and tools, 14
   techniques, 24
supplies, and materials, 10–16
   other, 16

T

tapered trailing, 42
thread painting, 45
   a menagerie, 148–181
   beginner creatures, 116–147
   tips for, 45–46
thread. **See** floss
threader, needle, 13
tools, pattern transfer, 15–16
tote bag, embroidery on, 49
trailing, 42
   tapered, 42
transfer tools, 15
tufted titmouse, 170
Turkey work, 43
   tip for, 43
tweezers, 16

V

variegated floss, 12
vines, 124

W

water-soluble fabric marker, 15, 16
waves, 66
wheatear stitch, 43
   fill, 44
whipped back stitch, 44
white gel pen, 15, 16
wire cutters, 14, 15
wire slips, 27
   creating, 27
wire tools, 14
wire, 14
   cotton-covered, 15
wool, natural, 15
   attaching, padding, 26
woven wheel rose, 44
   open, 38

About the Author

Jessica Long is an embroidery art designer and instructor based near Phoenix, Arizona, where she lives with her husband, son, and three cats. She has loved art and nature since she was a child. In college, she studied biology and dreamed of becoming a natural science illustrator. Ultimately, she began a more traditional career working in a biotech lab, but her love of the natural world never faded, and she continued to sketch and paint during her free time.

In 2016, Jessica picked up hand embroidery as a way to slow down, connect with her creativity, and reduce anxiety after the birth of her son. She started designing and selling her patterns to share her love of embroidery with other fiber art hobbyists. As her business grew, she was able to pivot her career, teaching at workshops and online through platforms, such as YouTube and Craftsy, and expanding her line of embroidery kits. Her goal is for her students to find the same joy and relaxation that she finds when creating art through hand embroidery.

Please enjoy her library of online videos and tutorials, visiting www.JessicaLongEmbroidery.com or following the QR code below.